PONTIUS
PILATE

PONTIUS PILATE

Deciphering a Memory

ALDO SCHIAVONE

Translated by
Jeremy Carden

LIVERIGHT PUBLISHING CORPORATION
A DIVISION OF W. W. NORTON & COMPANY
Independent Publishers Since 1923
New York | London

For information about permission to reproduce selections from this book,
write to Permissions, Liveright Publishing Corporation, a division of
W. W. Norton & Company, Inc., 500 Fifth Avenue, New York, NY 10110

For information about special discounts for bulk purchases, please contact
W. W. Norton Special Sales at specialsales@wwnorton.com or 800-233-4830

Manufacturing by Berryville Graphics
Book design by Ellen Cipriano Design
Production manager: Julia Druskin

Library of Congress Cataloging-in-Publication Data

Names: Schiavone, Aldo, author.
Title: Pontius Pilate : deciphering a memory / Aldo Schiavone ; translated by
Jeremy Carden.
Other titles: Ponzio Pilato. English
Description: New York : Liveright Publishing Corporation, 2017. | Includes
bibliographical references and index.
Identifiers: LCCN 2016056360 | ISBN 9781631492358 (hardcover)
Subjects: LCSH: Pilate, Pontius, active 1st century. |
Governors—Palestine—Biography. | Jesus Christ—Trial. | Jesus
Christ—Crucifixion. | Palestine—History—To 70 A.D.
Classification: LCC BS2520.P55 S3513 2017 | DDC 226/.092—dc23
LC record available at https://lccn.loc.gov/2016056360

Liveright Publishing Corporation,
500 Fifth Avenue, New York, N.Y. 10110
www.wwnorton.com

W. W. Norton & Company Ltd.
15 Carlisle Street, London W1D 3BS

1 2 3 4 5 6 7 8 9 0

CONTENTS

+

Introduction   7

1. One Night in the Month of Nisan   19
2. Roman Judaea and the Work of the Fifth Prefect   52
3. God and Caesar   96
4. The Destiny of the Prisoner   131
5. Into the Darkness   169

Sources and Historiography   187
Notes   209
Index   227

INTRODUCTION

†

1.

This book is a critical inquiry into the figure of Pontius Pilate, the Roman governor of Judaea in the thirties of the first century AD. According to Christian tradition, during his mandate and with his direct participation an event without equal in Western history took place in Jerusalem, unfolding in no more than a handful of hours: the condemnation and death of Jesus of Nazareth. Pilate's career, insofar as we can glimpse it, is thus situated at the point of contact—which he himself provoked in part—between two unique and extraordinary stories: that of the Roman Empire at the peak of its power and that of the Christian faith at the time of its beginnings. It is upon this intersection, on the handed-down descriptions of this encounter, their interpretations, and the ines-timable consequences, that much of our account hinges.

Pilate is the only historical character—whose existence cannot be doubted in any way—to whom the Gospel memory ascribes a dialogue with Jesus: the final, extreme act of the Master's preaching, with an enormous political and theological significance, made complete precisely by the presence and attitude of the governor. He would seem to have uttered and heard words, and performed and witnessed gestures, that have been with us ever since—phrases and behaviors destined to build cultural foundations and create boundary divisions, probably among the best known and most widely discussed in the legacy of the whole of antiquity.

But why is his profile enveloped by the Gospels themselves in a shadow that confuses and shrouds it, rendering its features irremediably undefined and elusive? What do the writings try to hide, even though they have proved to be remarkably and almost inescapably suggestive over the centuries? Attempting to answer these questions will be like the surprising and unexpected deciphering of an enigma, lying right in the heart of early Christianity, and of its most ancient irradiation, and it is the principal goal of our research. Both of them take us by some path or other to Pilate's behavior and motivations: to his years spent serving the empire, which left behind just a few, but not insignificant, traces. To a life on the fringes of—though not outside—the most important circuit of Roman power, yet one which would lead him to take a decision of incalculable magnitude, capable of shaping the future of the world, and reached, what's more, in a way that the Gospels recount as torn and contradictory, and which has ended up making ambiguity the dominant aspect of his portrait.

Judaea was a difficult region, but not for strictly military reasons. Immediately upon arrival, Pilate had found himself dealing with complex issues, all reducible to what we might describe as problems of cultural compatibility. The Mosaic religion represented an insuperable obstacle to the processes of imperial integration that Rome was successfully conducting in many other regions of the Mediterranean East. The conquerors had undertaken to guarantee the free profession of that faith, but at the same time were very concerned to ensure that such a demanding cult should not foment insubordination to their power—an arduous task, open to continual misunderstandings, because the Jewish religion had always had a marked political and "national" imprint. The relations of the imperial authorities with the local populations and aristocracies were knotty and fraught, and a few decades later would end in a bloodbath and the complete destruction of Jerusalem. The story we are about to tell is also the catastrophe of a hopeless intellectual incomprehension, yielding consequences that still impinge upon us today.

2.

For two thousand years Pilate has been a figure on the boundary between memory and history, like—albeit with a different equilibrium of the two planes each time—Romulus, or King Arthur, or Joan of Arc. In our case, the border line is between religious memory on one hand, and political historiography and political–philosophical writings on the other.

The Gospels are not books of history, nor are they intended to be. They are the great laboratories of Christian religious belief, which inaugurated a new model of literary communication, with a previously untested relationship between writing and oral tradition. And it is in these texts that we encounter Pilate, in relation to the death of Jesus—a theme of primary importance in their narrative strategies. We discover him above all in the Gospel of John, which, of the four, is undoubtedly the closest to the context of first-century Palestine: a fortunate coincidence.

History (and philosophy) were instead the concern of Josephus and Philo of Alexandria: two first-century intellectuals who wrote about Pilate in relation to affairs in Roman Judaea during the rule of Tiberius and Caligula, with Josephus also referring to the death of Jesus, in a famous passage long wrangled over by critics. Beyond that, nothing truly significant has come down to us, with a couple of relevant exceptions: a brief reference by Tacitus (also mentioning Jesus, and likewise much disputed) and an important epigraph discovered in Caesarea in the 1960s.

Our reconstruction will therefore largely be a kind of journey within early Christian memory, remaining all the time in the orbit of its highest point, the death of Jesus, which also lies—and not by accident—at the intersection between Gospel narrative and Judaeo-Roman historiography. In my interpretation, I have tried to draw fruitfully on both these nuclei: Christian remembrance and imperial history.

Religious recollection—in particular that of the Gospels—is oriented more heavily toward the meaning and theological understanding of the events to which it alludes, and to the defense of their value in the age of the teller, than to recording the past as such. Modern New Testament criticism, and studies about the functioning of ancient cultural memory, have taught us a good deal about these mechanisms. Compared to what looks to be the plane of historically ascertained events, religious memory may even resort to seemingly pure invention, if it furthers the pursuit of goals considered to be didactically and theologically essential; and the only coherence we can expect is that which is found within the thoughts, impressions, and behaviors recalled on each occasion. We must, however, not exaggerate the distance between history and memory. Every elaboration of memory, even the boldest one, has its own background scene, which always relates to a solid skeleton of events, just as every historical source, even those we regard as most reliable, presents the facts through the filter of a subjective representation. The difficulty lies in finding the right measure.

The death of Jesus comes, in the mirror of all four Gospels, as the culmination of his preaching and testimony—not a trauma that interrupts a path, but an event that completes and perfects it, and projects it toward the eternal. The binary reform of the original and very rigid biblical monotheism—the Father and the Son—is definitively established precisely in that episode, as is the mysterious relationship between God and time. The completion of the Trinity we know now would only be sanctioned at a later date, marking the fascinating magic of the number three in theological–philosophical architecture between Egypt, Greece, and India. And above all, that event, and the moments leading up to it, gave rise to the genetic nucleus of the political theology of the West—it was from this death that Christianity really began—on which Paul and Augustine would then start to work. Paul makes no specific reference to Pilate, while Augustine, in his *Lectures on the Gospel according to St. John,* mentions the prefect on various occasions, but without untangling any of the knots associated with the interpretation of his choices.

It has been authoritatively shown that the Gospels—irrespective of their historic reliability—cannot be shaped, by adding together their biographic kernels, into a unitary account of the life of Jesus, and that a choice is required in particular for John with respect to the Synoptics (Matthew, Mark, and Luke). I believe this is fundamentally correct, giving due weight to often incompatible structural differences. But in our case it has less value, because equally well grounded, in my view, is the hypothesis according to which a fairly detailed written account of the death of Jesus—stitching together different sources and testimony—preceded the writings that go under the name of the four evangelists, basically establishing itself as a model; and I take the view that this original layer influenced John as well, notwithstanding important variants.

In the Christian tradition—but also in Tacitus (who was generally well informed, as we shall see, on Judaean affairs), and in Josephus, who certainly had access to firsthand sources—the recollection of the Passion is associated with seven names: Judas, Annas, Caiaphas, Herod Antipas, Barabbas, Joseph of Arimathea, and Pilate. The first—the traitor apostle—is just a figure of memory, for whom there is no verifiable evidence on the plane of history. The same is true of Barabbas. The other five are historical

characters: the two Sadducee high priests at the head of the Sanhedrin (a Jewish council of elders), the tetrarch of Galilee, the
Roman prefect of the province of Judaea, and probably Joseph of
Arimathea. Of them all, the decisive role fell to Pilate. His would
be the final word regarding the prisoner's destiny.

The appraisal of his behavior, already not univocal in Christian memory, and the extent to which contingent circumstances
influenced it, has prompted endless clashes and rifts over the centuries, which encapsulate, even today, whole universes of ideas
and values. We are at the crossroads of two religions capable,
over the course of millennia, of accruing imposing resources—
intellectual, moral, and of collective identity. It is a crucial point
touched on continually, through which rivers of history, some of
them turbulent and bloody, would flow.

To whom is the "responsibility" of the Cross to be attributed?
To the Jews—the "deicide" people of Christian intransigence—
or the Romans? And consequently, what was Pilate's role really?
That of a despot? An accomplice? A bungler?

These are questions that have been molded by a very long
tradition, both Jewish and Christian, into unbending stereotypical polarities that admit no way out. Rather than dwell-
ing radically on their legitimacy, a vast amount of research has
sought, over the last two centuries, to offer reliable answers to
the alternatives they pose, presenting solutions increasingly in
line with modern historical criticism and the new knowledge
we have acquired about first-century Judaean and imperial
Roman reality (social, administrative, and legal) in the eastern
Mediterranean.

In this historiography there is a bit of everything: traces of remote prejudices, forms of ideological subjection, an overpowering sense of guilt following the nameless horror of the Shoah, serious philology and rigorous hermeneutics, apologetics, intuitions of great importance, clashes between opposing orthodoxies, more or less laudable attempts at religious reconciliation, efforts to shrug off old and unjust accusations—in a word, a mass from which it is hard to emerge. Literature has also tackled the theme, offering us, between the nineteenth and twentieth centuries, at least two memorable though very different Pilates: those of Anatole France and of Mikhail Bulgakov. The first, as an old man, has completely erased from an otherwise keen mind even the faintest trace of his encounter with Jesus; the second is magically suspended between metaphysical foreknowledge and the strict routine of his government duties.

It would be impossible to ignore the significance of such a body of material—though it must be said that the works devoted exclusively to Pilate are not great in number. Care will be taken to acknowledge the debts we owe to some of them in particular, both more and less recent.

We will try, however, to approach the theme as if for the first time, without setting ourselves any other end—either theological or political—than to describe and explain what might have happened: to unravel and tease out a reasonably solid thread from that slippery and fragmentary amalgam, at once tangled and lacunose, in which every plausible reconstruction seems to flounder. The more we are overwhelmed by the number of attempts lying behind us, the more we need to avoid being bogged down by them, and to eschew the dustiness of over-worn paths and of intentions that have nothing to do with recounting the past. In keeping with this undertaking, we will try to move closer to our subject by seeking to renew the freshness of an attention cultivated without obligations, for the sheer pleasure of relating the story and of interpretation—in solitude and in liberty.

PONTIUS
PILATE

1

ONE NIGHT IN THE
MONTH OF NISAN

☦

1.

Pilate was in Jerusalem that day. He had arrived—we do not know exactly when—from his customary residence in Caesarea, the administrative capital of Roman Judaea, situated in the northwest of the small province on the Mediterranean coast near the border with Syria.

Darkness was falling, and in a large room "furnished and ready," probably with couches and rugs, on the upper floor of a house that must not have been too far away from the governor's quarters, a group of wayfarers, who had also recently come to the city, were preparing their table. We are indebted to Mark and Luke for the preservation of this detail: an evident remnant of oral memory, transmitted in an early core of writing prior to the Gospels—irrelevant for the purpose of the narrative but authentic and precious—which has survived and come down to us on the thread of that first recollection. In the Marcan text the detail is combined with a likely shift of the date: but the error, perhaps voluntary, is the author's, not in the tradition he was drawing on.

At the head of the small band was a man whose name, Latinized, was Jesus of Nazareth; those in his company had been chosen by him as his most faithful disciples—he was in fact a religious preacher and a master of doctrine and life. The occasion would be remembered forever as their Last Supper.

The place where the diners gathered has not been reliably identified. One tradition dating to the fourth century situates it on the hill of Gareb (the New Zion of the Christians), in the southwest part of the city, where the building containing the "Cenacle" room can be found today. But bearing in mind the sequence of events, perhaps we need to think of a house closer to the banks of the Kidron, the rushing torrent that for a stretch ran parallel to the walls. Pilate, on the other hand, resided in the splendid palace built by Herod the Great, which overlooked the whole high plain from the promontory on the opposite side to the Antonia Fortress. Jerusalem then had around forty thousand inhabitants—a lot for an ancient city, especially in that region—but distances were short within the circle of fortifications.

Historians have performed complicated, even astronomical, calculations in an attempt to date that evening with precision. In all probability the year was 30, though a different one has been proposed by some (33 would be plausible, 31 less so, and 32 or 29 are even more unlikely). The month, without a doubt, was Nisan, according to the nomenclature of the Jewish calendar. The day is highly controversial, and depends on a count about which tradition disagrees: on the one hand the Synoptics, on the other John, whom I would regard as more reliable. In any case, pinpointing it was primarily of theological value, serving not so much to establish a chronology as to situate the event that was about to happen in relation to the ritual symbology of the Jewish calendar: in the immediate proximity of, or coinciding with, the Passover. It was probably the 13th, or, less likely, the 14th of the month (one should also bear in mind that in the Jewish calendar days are counted from one evening to the next): for us it would be the 6th of April—and therefore, accepting the hypothesis I believe to be the best, a Thursday.

It was the period of Pesach and the Feast of Unleavened Bread: important celebrations, distinct yet contiguous, which commemorated the exodus (and liberation) from Egypt, and the settling of the chosen people in the Promised Land. Jerusalem, as always for the occasion, was teeming with worshippers who had arrived from all over Palestine; not just from Judaea but from Samaria, Idumea, Galilee, and further afield as well. So the population swelled during the festivities: the city had been the spiritual center of Israel since very remote times, and housed the reconstructed Temple of Solomon (the so-called Second Temple, completed, according to tradition, in 515 BC), recently enlarged, again by Herod. No one able to make it would have forgone the privilege of being there for the ceremonies. That small group of followers, gathered at the supper table around their Master, was just a tiny part of a swarming, multiform crowd.

The Mosaic religion had long formed the connective fabric

of Jewish identity: a totalizing practice that encompassed every aspect of life, political included, and created a sense of belonging so strong as to determine an ethnic and cultural estrangement from neighboring populations. The Bible was the center of this, and of crucial importance. For the people of Israel it was not only the book of theological revelation, but also that of their own "national" construction, through the pact with God. No other people had anything like it.

This profound religious sentiment formed the basis of an intransigently defended identity that had apocalyptic overtones and an evident theocratic vocation (God alone could govern Israel), a cogent and uncompromising community bond with a rare degree of intensity. In the civilizations of the ancient Mediterranean perhaps only Rome would develop an equally marked sense of self-recognition, with respect to the other Italic peoples; but it was tempered by a no less accentuated (and apparently contradictory) tendency toward inclusion and openness. An incandescent and foreboding resemblance existed between conquered and conquerors: Jews and Romans, a small people and a large empire, though in the case of Rome religion played a less invasive role in preserving this sharp self-perception, and we must look in other directions to explain the phenomenon.

We have reason to believe that it was customary for Pilate to travel up from Caesarea—a journey of no more than about seventy miles—for the festivals, as part of his routine duties. Judaea was not a large province, but it was restless, riven by constant tensions and unquelled insurrectional impulses, with the Roman presence far from being accepted as it was elsewhere in the empire and in the East itself. Just a few decades later the contrasts would explode in an extremely violent revolt, stifled only with considerable difficulty and bloodshed: the second wave of the Diaspora.

So, on sensitive days like those of Pesach—characterized by congregating masses who must to Roman eyes have seemed dangerously prone to sudden outbursts of religious irredentist fanaticism—it was normal for the prefect to be on the spot to maintain a close watch and control. He may also have had to attend to ordinary justice. Roman governors were accustomed to moving around the main cities of the territory assigned to them in order to carry out their judicial responsibilities, a practice that would later be rigidly disciplined by the imperial administration and by jurists. Pilate might have taken advantage of the occasion to carry out two equally important tasks at the same time.

That year—whether it was 30 or 33—there were no particular threats to public order to worry him. The situation seemed relatively calm.

But it was still necessary to be vigilant, and to stifle any trouble at once. Pilate knew only too well that the military presence he could rely on in the event of an emergency was far from imposing. Unlike the nearby province of Syria, a much vaster and more exposed region, where as many as four legions were available to the imperial legate—the VI "Ferrata," the X "Fretensis," the III "Gallica," and, from 18, the XII "Fulminata"—Pilate probably had no more than a unit of cavalry (an *"ala I gemina Sebastenorum,"* roughly a regiment) and five cohorts of infantry: one of these may have been Roman, while the others would have been recruited locally (but not from among the Jews, who were exempt from service) and commanded by officers of Eastern origin. Most of these troops were quartered in Caesarea. In Jerusalem, in the imposing Antonia Fortress close to the Temple, there was as a rule just one cohort (between five hundred and a thousand men) supported by a small cavalry detachment, under the orders of a tribune and with policing functions. Several extra units might have been deployed to the city when the governor was in residence, camped in Herod's palace and the immediate vicinity, but the numbers involved would have been small. Prudence cautioned against larger forces: their presence in places sacred to the faith of the Jews would have been seen as an unjustified provocation. And anyway, this was the Roman strategy: wherever possible, to make a gossamer administration and a handful of men suffice, to govern more by consensus than by arms.

Nor was this the first time that Jesus had gone up to Jerusalem (as John writes), though the Synoptics mention no other journeys. We cannot say how many times he had previously been there: it depends on the duration we attribute to his public life—no less than two years and no more than four.

On this occasion, he had been in the city since the previous Sunday (the start of the Jewish week); he had arrived on the back of a young ass, greeted and acclaimed by a crowd of curious onlookers and cheering followers holding palm fronds. He had spent the following days preaching in the Temple, talking, engaging, arguing even; his fame had grown greatly. Everything suggests that Jesus was now a well-known and talked-about figure from Galilee to Judaea, at the center of a lot of attention, and not just of the people: a character who was emerging from among the galaxy of preachers, prophets, and magic-workers who travelled tirelessly from one end of first-century Palestine to the other, rendering feverish and overwrought the religious yearnings of its people.

2.

Pilate had agreed to have Jesus arrested that evening. It was to be conducted as a rapid surprise action, a kind of nocturnal *coup de main,* and we cannot rule out that the operation was a further reason for him to stay over in Jerusalem.

How had he come to make this choice?

That the governor knew what was afoot goes without question. The course of events during the night makes it certain, offering us (as we shall see) almost direct proof. And even though it is always wise to mistrust reasoning which concludes with the words "he couldn't not have known"—usually the last resort of those without other arguments—in this case, it must be conceded, that is exactly how it was: it would have been impossible for him not to be informed.

A more difficult task, at first sight, would seem to be the appraisal of Pilate's direct involvement in the decision. It is very likely, indeed almost certain, that the idea was not originally his. The Gospels—which on this essential point evidently reflect their shared source on the Passion—attribute it without hesitation to the Jewish priestly aristocracy, and contextualize the final planning of it in the last days spent by Jesus in Jerusalem, when his behavior and words looked on more than one occasion to be an open challenge to the city's religious authorities. "When the chief priests and the scribes heard it [the driving out of the traders from the temple], they kept looking for a way to kill him; for they were afraid of him, because the whole crowd was spellbound by his teaching," writes Mark.

But it is equally certain that if Pilate had wanted to prevent, or at least to postpone, even indefinitely, the hastening of events, he had full power to do so. He represented Roman political power in Judaea, a province of the empire, and nothing important to the maintenance of order could happen without his consent. The Jewish authorities enjoyed considerable autonomy regarding criminal repression on religious issues, but public security was a wholly Roman affair. The arrest, after all, was not a trifling matter: it was a question of stopping a man who had become very popular, with a following hard to contain. The last few days had confirmed it: from Jesus's triumphal entry into the city ("the whole city was in turmoil, asking, 'Who is this?'" Matthew says), to the harsh clash with the religious community leaders that he had not wished to mitigate: "The chief priests and the scribes were looking for a way to put Jesus to death, for they were afraid of the people," we read in Luke.

Pilate, then, was not just informed about but shared in the decision—and, as we shall see, his involvement was much greater than that.

JESUS KNEW WHAT AWAITED HIM. His whole life had been a long preparation for this moment—an impassioned search for what he felt was the only path that would take him back to the Father. It was the moment of his glorification, as John says. And though Christian memory may well have retrospectively emphasized, for evident theological and scriptural reasons, the force and clarity of the premonition, it is reasonable to suppose that, by choosing to return to Jerusalem for the festivities, Jesus was consciously stepping into a trap from which he would not reemerge.

The whole supper had been an early and painful farewell: "The hour . . . has come, when . . . you will leave me alone," recounts John. A dramatic leavetaking, barely lightened by the promise of a future reunion. It is the leading motif of the Passion, repeated, albeit from different perspectives, in all the Gospels. The design of the Father, reflected in the mind of he who, while considering himself his Son, had human feelings, could not but itself be reduced to a human dimension, and hence be clouded by uncertainty and doubt: transformed into emotion and mystery, cracked by intermittency, anguish, dismay. Of the four, Luke is perhaps the most attentive to the density of Jesus's existential condition— that of the historic Jesus—at the moment of his greatest test.

It is now deep into the night. The Master leaves the house of his host, and with his supper companions soon reaches a place familiar to him, a smallholding across the Kidron valley, near the Mount of Olives: the grove or garden of Gethsemane. It is his habit to spend the night outside the city. He then moves a few paces away from his disciples ("a stone's throw," writes Luke), who have not understood (or not wanted to), despite the words they have just heard, the gravity of the moment. They are tired, distracted, gloomy. They sleep.

Jesus remains wakeful and prays in the dark, "distressed and agitated." Shortly before, he had said to Peter, John, and James, whom he wanted close to him, "I am deeply grieved, even to death," while, Luke tells us, "his sweat became like great drops of blood falling down on the ground." He would like to ward off what is about to happen: "Father, if you are willing, remove this cup from me," he asks. This last sentence is a literary invention—though we do not know whose. Jesus is alone now, and no one would have heard him, even granting that he was praying aloud. And in the darkness of the night no one could have seen the transformation of his sweat—a rare occurrence, though physiologically not impossible in particularly acute and prolonged conditions of stress—if, that is, Luke's image had more than merely metaphorical meaning.

At any rate, the suffering and woe—the extreme tension of Jesus's psychological state—had been evident during and after the supper, and subsequent events would explain the reasons and fix the image in early Christian memory. Understandably, Mark, Matthew, and above all Luke project this mental state onto Jesus's last moments of liberty. Under the weight of the catastrophe he sensed was imminent, in their account the human and divine are torn apart in the Master: the two planes become detached in a sea of suffering—where everything, confounded, vacillates—and seem unable to coincide anymore.

The wait does not last much longer. The trap is sprung. The garden is surrounded by armed men with torches. There is no escape.

The operation had been planned with some care. Both the Synoptics and John, as we have seen, preserve more than a trace of the progressive machination. The darkness and the secluded location were ably exploited to avoid indiscreet eyes and any attempt by the people to defend the quarry—a constant worry for the priests.

The men who closed in on Jesus to carry out the arrest answered to the Sanhedrin, and were backed up by a squad of the so-called temple police, a permanent unit generally responsible for guarding and quelling disturbances in and around the place of worship. Equipped in a fairly makeshift fashion (the Gospels speak of clubs), they were probably poorly trained as well—which would explain a certain commotion at the moment of capture, despite the careful planning.

With them that night, though not in the front line and therefore not in direct contact with the wanted man, was a detachment of Roman troops.

The Synoptics do not mention this presence, much disputed by historians, who have even gone so far as to deny it, or, for opposing and symmetrical reasons, to ascribe an excessive role to the Romans. It is John who specifically refers to them, and there is no reason not to trust him, while we can explain Luke's silence by his tendency to assume a pro-Roman attitude regarding responsibility for the martyrdom; as for the versions of Mark and Matthew, they are much more cursory on this point, although we cannot rule out a deliberate omission.

The imperial force was substantial, its deployment revealing that the entire operation had been directed by the Roman authorities. John alludes with precision and a careful choice of words to a cohort, commanded by its tribune—which would amount to the whole normal garrison of Jerusalem. This is probably an exaggeration (though the coincidence is significant, and enhances the credibility of the account), prompted by a wish to stress the Roman involvement. It is more likely to have been a smaller force, perhaps a maniple, though under the orders of the tribune in person (specifically mentioned by John). The Romans' task was evidently not to carry out the actual arrest, which seems to be ruled out by the sequence of events, despite an ambiguous sentence in John—who was listing the participants in the action, rather than indicating those making the arrest—but to cover the operation and ensure that no public disorder broke out due to Jesus's popularity, which may have been prudently overestimated. We can imagine it to have been a fairly complex plan of action, undoubtedly devised by professionals, and therefore by the Romans: an almost military-style maneuver, with the imperial troops deployed to block access to the area, according to the protocol for a siege, and the temple police in the vanguard, with the job of apprehending and delivering the wanted man to the authorities.

IF THIS WAS INDEED THE SITUATION on the ground—and the reconstruction is reasonable, arranging the available information in the most sensible way—it gives us further and decisive evidence of Pilate's involvement. It is unthinkable that a significant contingent of troops, led by the garrison commander himself, would leave the Antonia Fortress on a delicate nighttime mission without having received precise instructions. The governor knew about the plan, had probably discussed the more strictly military aspects (timing, location) with the tribune, and had given his approval for a joint police intervention, in which local forces acted within a protective screen of imperial troops.

And that is not all. We have good grounds for supposing something further—that the entire operation was conceived and then executed on the basis of an explicit understanding between the prefect and the Jewish religious authorities, an agreement evidently pressed for by the priests (impossible to think otherwise) and representing the culmination of their design: to involve the Romans in the elimination of Jesus, to use them as a shield against the populace, whose reaction, as we have seen, they feared.

They would thus have tried to impress upon Pilate the danger Jesus posed for public order in the province. In his activities (this must have been their argument—we will return to it), scandalous religious preaching—which the high priests should in any case have repressed on their own, as they had the faculty to do—had openly spilled over into political instigation. The matter no longer concerned only the Jewish authorities, but the Roman ones as well. The issue had moved onto another plane. Getting rid of the troublemaker was a primary common interest. The priests were playing it clever, their aim being to achieve a small political masterpiece: to make use of the Romans to obtain a result advantageous for themselves alone. There was nothing novel in this. In the protracted wrestling matches between the imperial authorities and provincial aristocracies, especially in the East— where recognition and power were continually granted in return for consensus—there was plenty of scope for such ploys.

The prefect's initial response was probably quite cautious. Perhaps he did not have reliable firsthand information about Jesus, or at least not enough. He did not greatly trust the priests, despite long familiarity with their chief, and feared a false step, maybe even a trap. Still, he hesitated to refuse them. Jesus really might be dangerous; and nor did he want to displease his petitioners. For now the Jews could be allowed to bring Jesus in, acting on the basis of local self-determination in religious affairs—and also of the repression of related crimes—supported at a distance by the Roman presence. But before the prefect interrogated—and possibly also condemned—the presumed subversive, the Sanhedrin would have to assume the public responsibility of formulating a specific charge, valid on the yardstick of imperial justice: Jesus would have to be regarded as the perpetrator not only of a religious misdeed, but of a political plot as well. Until that crime was publicly proclaimed, the Romans would not touch the prisoner.

This explanation is, I must stress, purely conjectural. But no other reconstruction accounts for the course of events. If the idea of the arrest had originally been Roman—as has been argued—the prefect could have done it himself: he had no need of a Jewish presence to justify it, far less of the temple guards. And once Jesus was captured, it is unthinkable that the soldiers of the cohort would have done anything other than immediately lock the prisoner in the fortress to await his summons by Pilate. The only way to explain the joint participation, Roman and Jewish, in the operation, with the arrest being made by the Jewish guard unit who then kept the prisoner, is to suppose that the original initiative came from the priests, aided by the Romans, who for the moment remained in the background, waiting for the situation to become clearer.

As for the extreme idea, which has also been floated, that the Jewish guard turned out—armed!—in an attempt to wrest Jesus away from the Romans, this seems totally unlikely. The imperial troops would not have tolerated any interference by armed men in the zone of one of their operations, and the unauthorized presence of the Jewish guard far from the Temple would have been seen as a challenge or an act of open revolt, and as such deserving of an adequate response. All opposition would have been swept away instantly.

There is no other possibility: the arrest must be considered a Jewish intervention, conducted with the active consent of the Roman prefect. A precarious interplay was thus wrought between imperial decision (in the hands of the governor) and the local religious aristocracy (represented by the high priest) on the basis of their respective competences: political and religious. The boundaries between the two components, Roman and Jewish—so different in mentality, culture, and objectives, and far from trustful of each other—could not but present a wide margin for uncertainty, as would soon be seen.

ALSO PARTICIPATING IN THE EXECUTION of the plan, according to the Gospels, which on this point are unanimous, was a traitor—one of Jesus's apostles—who led the Roman–Jewish forces to the right spot and helped to identify the wanted man.

The figure of Judas belongs to Christian memory alone, and is not borne out on the plane of history. Yet there is no reason to believe he was an invention of the Gospels, constructed to further highlight the abandonment Jesus would experience, with duplicity and deceit worming their way even into his inner circle. It is better to view the disciple's betrayal as part of the more ancient oral tradition surrounding the death of Jesus and then of the common source used for the Passion story, and for this reason present in all the Gospels. It was, as it were, a constitutive element of the original "realism" of the narrative, and should be considered as such by us.

As soon as he arrived in Jerusalem, the unfaithful disciple (so the story goes) went to the priests in secret; evidently he had been thinking about this betrayal for some time, and neither their hostility toward Jesus nor (probably) their aims had escaped him. He offered to hand over the Master, an important piece of help in the execution of the plan; and it is plausible that the information precipitated the arrest, dispelling lingering hesitations.

Until then no one had expressed doubts about the apostle. Only Jesus, during the supper, had shown awareness of his intentions, even exhorting him to get on with the betrayal ("Do quickly what you are going to do," records John): words which deepen—especially in Matthew's account—the gloomy atmosphere of the moment, emphasizing Jesus's heartbreaking and foreboding solitude.

The reasons for Judas's conduct are obscure; none of the Gospels say a single word about them. It is hard to believe it was just a question of money, though money is something with which Judas must have been avidly familiar (he had already stolen from the kitty entrusted to his care). The reward he would obtain was modest, perhaps no more than the usual sum paid out by the Jewish authorities for such deals, and it is difficult to imagine this alone led him to take such an extreme step.

At any rate, in the dynamics of that night's events the presence of a spy does not appear at all out of the ordinary, just as it does not in the preparatory phase of the Roman–Jewish plan. Informers were an essential part of the capillary nature of imperial control over the territory, especially in the large cities. It is plausible that before moving out in force the Romans wanted to be sure about the timing and location, and that the priests had guaranteed fresh and reliable information—of the kind only Judas could supply, from within Jesus's innermost circle—almost in real time.

WHEN THE JEWISH GUARD—who had perhaps identified their quarry with Judas's help—moved in, Jesus had regained his composure and appeared to be perfectly in control of himself. He would remain so to the end. The momentary crack in his resolve while praying had been overcome, dispelled by his full identification with what he perceived, once again clearly, as the will of the Father. The intermittence had ended, the human and the divine plane reunited once more in the feelings of the Son.

Jesus—in John's account—faces the men coming toward him

with calm pride. He asks them who they are looking for, and when they say his name, he does not hesitate to identify himself and submit to them, asking that in return his companions be left alone. The disciples are awake by now. Someone attempts to respond. A guard ("the high priest's servant," writes John) is wounded by a sword, perhaps Peter's. Jesus orders an immediate halt to all resistance. Luke does not explain this choice (and there is not even any mention of the episode in Mark). In Matthew and John we find two different interpretations, which, however, may not rule each other out. The first is a repudiation of violence ("all who take the sword will perish by the sword"), and is no surprise. The second, John's, is more unexpected: "Put your sword back into its sheath. Am I not to drink the cup that the Father has given me?"—an evident and lapidary reference to the ineluctability of his human destiny. Jesus is certain that nothing will now spare him from death, and above all that nothing should be tried, by anyone, to do so. We must keep this state of mind in our heads. It will be useful further on.

"Have you come out with swords and clubs as if I were a bandit?" he says sorrowfully to the armed men. They capture him, and probably bind him. The disciples flee in the darkness. No one follows them. The operation only envisaged one arrest.

We can suppose that Pilate was still up, in his residence, waiting for a report. Anything different would be surprising: there were Roman units in the field, and in Jerusalem at that, during the sensitive festive days.

Good news arrived almost straightaway: Roman organization, when it came to conveying information efficiently, was flawless. Everything had gone according to plan. The surprise move had been successful and the arrest made without mishap; the prisoner was now in the hands of the priests, as agreed.

All around, the city was quiet, enveloped in sleep. The troops returned to the fortress. For the prefect of Judaea, the night could be regarded as over.

3.

The priests' plan, agreed to by the Romans, was for Jesus to be immediately moved away from the arrest site and taken without delay, by the same people who had captured him, to a secure location in Jerusalem, not far from Pilate's residence. And that is what happened.

The solution they chose, as John recounts, seems to have been the house of Annas, son of Seth, the authoritative father-in-law of the high priest then in office, Caiaphas, and a former high priest himself between the years 6 and 15. Annas had been appointed to that post by the legate of Syria, Publius Sulpicius Quirinius. The Roman governors—of Syria or of Judaea—had arrogated this important power to themselves, and exercised it by choosing from among the Sadducee aristocracy; this was intended to ensure a certain degree of meek collaboration with the imperial authorities by the Jewish elite. Annas had been removed by Valerius Gratus, Pontius Pilate's immediate predecessor in the prefecture of Judaea, upon his arrival in Caesarea in 15. Josephus describes the priest (whom he calls Ananos) as a "happy" man, the father of five sons who had all, in turn, become high priests—something which had never happened before, the historian notes. It was a rich and powerful aristocratic family, of old and consolidated prestige. His residence is thought to have been in the southeast part of the city, possibly in the same palace where Caiaphas lived. Jesus, now a prisoner and with a heavy escort (only Jewish, we can suppose), would therefore have covered, in reverse, more or less the same route he had taken to Gethsemane a few hours earlier.

What happens next is not entirely clear, and has led to lengthy discussion among scholars. Many of them—in particular, historians of ancient laws—have fallen into what I consider to be a deforming and stubborn formalistic prejudice, namely, that the only key to reconstructing the events is to place them within the paradigm of the "trial" of Jesus—first Jewish, then Roman. According to this interpretation, it would be entirely reasonable to suppose that, after his capture, Jesus underwent a regular trial, or at least something very similar to a regular trial: first by the religious authorities of Jerusalem and then in the court of the Roman prefect, the former on the basis of Jewish law, the latter in compliance with Roman law. Some have even ventured to hypothesize the existence of a unitary procedure with two distinct phases, separate but connected: Jewish and Roman. In any case, even without going so far, the end result is a projection onto Jewish cultural and institutional reality—where every function we describe as "legal" was actually integrated, with no autonomy, into the religious apparatus, and what we call a "trial" was in effect a theocratic celebration—of models that were quite extraneous to it, that is to say, those familiar to us from the history of

Roman law, in which the procedures of criminal repression—at least as far as citizens were concerned—had already undergone a lengthy elaboration that we can rightly call "legal" in the strict sense of the term. Consequently, the Gospel stories—both the Synoptics and John—were forced into the preestablished scheme of the "trial": and when things did not add up (which was almost always), all sorts of expedients were adopted without hesitation—pressure on texts, legalistic captiousness, historically improbable reasoning—so as to bring out, around Jesus, the forms and content of an activity that could be defined (according to our paradigms) as properly "judicial."

I believe that the narratives available to us point in a very different direction. It would be interesting to see when and in precisely which cultural environment the myth of the "trial" of Jesus, already perfectly formed by the seventeenth century, took root; it seems to carry a strong influence of medieval legal culture, a mix of theology and canonic law, intended to press Jesus's earthly destiny into the magnetic field of a legal mindset implacable and punctilious in its pursuit of injustice, a kind of extreme *summum ius, summa iniuria*—the height of law, the height of injustice. But this is another issue, which we cannot develop here.

Let us consider the events of the first few hours after the capture.

Jesus arrived in the house of Annas no earlier than midnight, perhaps later. Without a doubt he was expected, both by Annas and by his son-in-law Caiaphas, the high priest in office, appointed by Valerius Gratus in 18 or 19, mentioned by Josephus. (His tomb has probably been found recently in an ancient cemetery in south

Jerusalem.) His real name was Joseph; Caiaphas was just the name he went by, as often used to be the custom. He too had solid Sadducee aristocratic origins. Born in the years of Herod—exactly when is unclear—he had married one of Annas's daughters, whose name we do not know, a matrimonial strategy that favored his career, linking him to an even more important family that had long been at the top of the community. His spell in office was unusually long: it lasted until 36, when he was removed by the legate of Syria, Vitellius. It is inconceivable that Pilate accepted Caiaphas's presence throughout his mandate without there having been some kind of regular collaboration, albeit within the limits made inevitable by their cultural diversity. It can reasonably be supposed that the two priests themselves had discussed with Pilate the plan to arrest Jesus, if it was Caiaphas who said, as John recalls, "that it is better . . . to have one man die for [the salvation of] the people." We will return to this sentence.

Envisaging the imminent capture, Caiaphas had urgently called together the members of the Sanhedrin: a council of seventy-one notables, both Pharisees and Sadducees—priests, scribes, and elders, according to the description of Josephus, who confirms the Gospels—of an evident theocratic stamp; its tasks were varied, and included those of a court, though strictly within the boundaries of the administrative autonomy conceded by the Romans. Considerable uncertainty surrounds the assembly's functions in the years that concern us, while some even doubt—though I am not convinced we need go so far—that it continued to exist formally after Judaea was reduced to the status of an imperial province. At any rate, it is highly improbable that a convocation during the night, or at the latest, in the very first light of dawn, in Caiaphas's house and on the day preceding the Passover, would have resembled an official session, held to conduct something similar to what we would describe as a trial, with even summary respect for Jewish laws. Had it taken that form, it would have glaringly violated the religious prescriptions in essential respects: the meeting was held outside the Temple area; it took place at night rather than in the daytime, and during a festive period; and it included none of the rituals prescribed for testimonial evidence.

In fact, as we have seen, a "trial," or anything like it, is not mentioned in any of the Gospels. John's account (considered by many scholars to display a textual incongruence on this point) does not even make any reference to the meeting. Luke describes the priests interrogating Jesus at dawn, ending with their finding him to be evidently guilty. Matthew reports a fairly chaotic interrogation, at which witnesses willing to speak against Jesus are heard. Even Mark's version, usually adduced as proof of the existence of a "sentence," only says this if the reading of the passage is forced. If we look at it with eyes free from prejudice, we realize it proves nothing; there is not even a need to suppose a falsification of the original text.

There is nothing to do but admit it: in none of the sources available to us is there any mention of a formal verdict—only of an accusation shared by those present, and the forming of a widespread conviction as to Jesus's guilt, induced also (and perhaps above all) by his own behavior. It is hard to describe this as a trial, quite aside from the further and not insignificant problem of our lack of information about the Jewish framework of rules for repressing religious crimes during Jesus's time. Rather, all the clues point to an agitated session of a council of elders held in a state of exception—in a private house, however prestigious, between late night and dawn—in order to quickly formulate a charge demanded without delay by the Romans as a prerequisite for intervening, and which could not be refused.

WE CAN NOW PROPOSE a plausible reconstruction, which does not interpose any preconceptions between the texts and our reading.

After Jesus arrived in the residence of Annas, his first encounter would definitely have been with the master of the household. Before that—along the way and while waiting for the priest—he had probably been ill-treated: he was blindfolded (according to Luke) and then showered with insults, derision, and blows by the guards and the servants who were camped in the courtyard and all around the house, perhaps also for security reasons. It was a cold night, and a fire had been lit. Peter, who had followed Jesus at a distance with another of the disciples, went to stand with these men; it was on this occasion that he denied his Master three times, repeatedly declaring he had nothing to do with him.

The atmosphere around the prisoner was heavy and intimidating. With his arrest and the flight of his companions, it was as if the charisma which until that moment had enveloped and protected Jesus, ensuring his inviolability, had dissolved, at least for those who had taken part in—or witnessed—the nocturnal expedition. The capture had broken the spell—irreversibly, for that night. Peter must have perceived the unexpected rapidity of the change with particular acuteness. His thrice-repeated denial marks the time of the whole sequence with an unforgettable and reiterated dramatic cadence. Jesus's teaching seemed to be ending in complete disaster. From now on he would be alone, and totally at the mercy—above all, physical—of his persecutors.

An interrogation by Annas is spoken of only by John, though he says nothing about a meeting of the Sanhedrin. In the Synoptics, on the other hand, Caiaphas has Jesus brought before the council straight away, and there is no trace of preliminary questioning either by him or by Annas.

The two versions do not rule each other out; they can be integrated. First of all, it must be said that an interrogation by Annas without a subsequent session in front of the council (John's version) makes no sense. Bringing Jesus before the father-in-law of the high priest, however powerful and influential he was, would have been pointless. Pilate must necessarily have demanded something different: a collectively formulated charge, not a conspiracy of priests. The only logical explanation for the whole dynamic of that night, and its precedents, is the need to bring Jesus—prior to handing him over to the Romans—in front of an assembly deemed in Roman eyes to represent the religious sentiment of the whole community. Annas, on his own, would not have been enough.

On the other hand, it is also likely that, before the decisive meeting, Annas, and perhaps Caiaphas himself, wanted an immediate and more discreet session with the prisoner, to gauge his reactions and probe his state of mind. A decision would have to be made about what to do next, when the council met, and any information obtained, as it were, firsthand might prove indispensable. A certain amount of time—perhaps hours—would in any case have gone by between the arrival of the captive Jesus and that of a sufficient number of council members, who would have been summoned without much warning (also to keep the operation secret) and would have arrived in dribs and drabs, once again under cover of darkness.

So Annas questions Jesus, perhaps already with Caiaphas present: rather vehemently, we can suppose. They are not alone. There are guards, and probably also someone to transcribe their words. They ask him, so John says, about his disciples and his teaching. It is not a trial, and is not described as such. Yet it is vaguely reminiscent of one, and that beginning has something sadly familiar about it, however completely out of context. It recalls the start of an Inquisition procedure in Europe between the medieval and early modern age.

Jesus responds memorably, with courage and ability: "I have spoken openly to the world; I have always taught in synagogues and in the temple, where all the Jews come together. I have said nothing in secret. Why do you ask me? Ask those who heard . . .: they know what I said." In his reply, the situation is overturned: the reasons for the secretive, nighttime inquiry simply do not hold up. There is nothing to investigate. He sets the light of the preached word against the darkness of secret machination. The enormity of the arrest can no longer be masked. The whole world is called as a witness, and that barely evoked presence suffices to illuminate and knock down every improvised prison. Jesus's teaching has always been directed at the entire community, and through it, at every woman and every man on Earth. Everyone has heard it, in the synagogues and in the Temple. There is no need for any inquiry or any checking of his doctrine. The universality of his teaching disrupts the relations of force, bringing the accused—free—back into the center of the scene.

The inquisitor is thrown off balance. Probably he falls silent. He did not expect such a vigorous reply. The questioning is interrupted. It gives way to violence: one of the guards strikes the prisoner, saying, "Is that how you answer the high priest?" At this point Jesus turns his attention away from Annas and addresses the man who has hit him: "If I have spoken wrongly, testify to the wrong. But if I have spoken rightly, why do you strike me?" He is no longer interested in the dialogue with the priest, the imposture of the inquiry having been revealed. Now it is the arbitrariness of the physical abuse he wishes to denounce, when it seeks to replace argument and fill the void with humiliation and belittlement.

John adds nothing more. The questioning was clearly less brief than these two replies indicate, and perhaps more blows and intimidation followed. But his narrative purpose is not to summarize or present the minutes of a hearing. It revolves around a single theme: to render evident the ability of Jesus, through his behavior and answers, to reveal, step by step, the mystificatory nature of the apparatus that was crushing him: the speciousness of the inquiry and the unreasoning arbitrariness of the violence.

This choice—it seems to me—also explains why John passed over the subsequent meeting of the Sanhedrin, even if, as seems likely, he had found traces of it in his source. According to the perspective adopted in the account, what needed to be remembered about that night—namely, the attempt to put together an indictment, and Jesus's composed force in overturning, in dramatic circumstances, the accusations leveled against him by the Jewish authorities—had already been said. After Annas's questioning no "sentence" was passed that necessarily had to be reported, nor any ritual performed about which silence could not be kept. Even less, for that narrative method, was there an obligation of completeness to respect. The story could move on, and go directly to the climax of the drama. Certainly, the structure of the narrative ends up being compromised from a strictly historical point of view, because (as we have already noted) the transfer of Jesus to the residence of Annas and Caiaphas cannot be justified without an appearance before the council. But these were not concerns for the person who composed that version. He—and his assumed readers—cared about things other than historical coherence.

LET US NOW LEAVE JOHN and follow the reconstruction of the Synoptics, which have a common narrative structure, albeit with some divergences.

It cannot have been long before dawn when Jesus was taken to Caiaphas's palace (which, as we have said, was perhaps a wing of the same building where Annas lived). Gathered together here, by then, was a significant part, probably the majority, of the Sanhedrin. They knew full well who was about to be brought before them. In the previous weeks they had convened to decide what to do with Jesus; a trace of such a meeting can be found in all four Gospels—going back to their shared source—and it was on this occasion, according to John, that Caiaphas said (as we have just noted) that it was better for one man to die so the people did not perish.

This is, for us, a very important declaration, because it reveals the line taken by the high priest and adopted by the Sanhedrin: the shifting of Jesus's misdeeds from the religious to the political plane, in order to involve Pilate. His words voiced the view that Jesus's preaching represented a threat for all the people of Israel; its subversive content would stir up the populace against the Romans, provoking a disastrous repression. The strategy already contained the suggestion that could be presented to the Roman governor: Jesus is a dangerous fomenter of disorder; he is no longer just a religious but also a political problem. He must be stopped as soon as possible, before he does more damage.

Jesus was brought before the assembly and questioned once again. The meeting did not last long. The decision had already been taken. But the machination had to end where it had started.

We have two versions of this epilogue: that of Luke and that of Mark (from which Matthew's almost certainly derives).

Luke's account revolves around two questions the prisoner seems to have been asked by those present, probably coached by Caiaphas. First: tell us who you are. Then, following Jesus's allusive but equivocal reply—"If I tell you, you will not believe; and if I question you, you will not answer. But from now on the Son of Man will be seated at the right hand of the power of God"—they insist: "Are you . . . the Son of God?" And here Jesus responds: "You say that I am." The rupture is complete. Any possibility of mediation on the part of the assembly—even granted that there was still time—was irreversibly lost. An unclosable distance suddenly opens up between the men of the Sanhedrin and the person in front of them: a genuine abyss, which makes it unthinkable to continue the inquisition. And in fact the notables say only, "What further testimony do we need? We have heard it ourselves from his own lips!" Up to this point, Luke has made no mention of the Sanhedrin searching for witnesses. He does so only now, with a very effective ellipsis, to convey its uselessness from the assembly's point of view, having heard the words of Jesus. The inquiry is over. There is no formal pronouncement. But the council members are convinced a man such as this can no longer remain either free or alive. The conspiracy is out in the open, and has become a pronouncement in the name of Israel. The assembly rises. It is now morning. The prisoner—still in chains—is taken to Pilate.

The much more lively scene described by Mark centers on the assembly's hearing of witnesses so as to formulate a charge against Jesus: the Lucan reference we just mentioned finds its explanation here. Who were these people? Other men summoned in the night, and kept in the wings waiting for Jesus? In theory, things might have gone like that. But how many were there? "Many," says Mark. Could a lot of witnesses have been called? It is hard to believe. And if so, how were they chosen? Had they already been questioned, to hear what they had to say? And by whom? But even if things had gone like that, one would at this point expect any testimony to have been manipulated—selected and rehearsed beforehand—and held ready to be produced as required. But according to Mark, the witnesses were not in agreement, and could not be taken into consideration.

How can we overcome these significant incongruences? I suggest that the voices raised against Jesus, as we read in Mark, were not—at least not all of them—those of witnesses from outside the council, but members of the Sanhedrin itself who, with some confusion—absolutely explainable, given the time and inevitable commotion—stood up to accuse the prisoner of various religious crimes.

An intersecting barrage of declarations levelled against Jesus by those present, most from within and a few from outside the Sanhedrin, is ultimately the most plausible hypothesis. This would also explain a sentence in Matthew ("At last two came forward"), which seems to refer explicitly to the presence of at least a couple of witnesses from outside the council; it is quite possible that a few—but not the "many" of Mark—had been summoned. Still, it is also credible that Matthew simply misunderstood Mark's text (or his source), and interpreted it in the sense of giving substance to the presence of witnesses who did not actually exist.

This reading would be untenable if the Sanhedrin had met as a court, to conduct what we would call a regular trial. But—I repeat—nothing of what we know points in that direction, and we must consider the tangle that has emerged as another indication of the difficulties we run into if we try to superimpose onto the events of that night the scheme of the "trial" of Jesus. What took place in those convulsive hours was not a court proceeding, but an emergency meeting of a theocratic body, preceded by a cursory inquisition by a high priest, with the aim of transforming a barely hatched conspiracy into a political–religious charge which, legitimately advanced in the name of Israel, could be acted upon by Pilate.

The testimony—whoever gave it—led to nothing. Jesus did not answer, and perhaps this silence is more plausible if the accusations came from members of the Sanhedrin, to whom the prisoner had nothing more to say, than if they came from new voices, to whom he might have felt the need to reply.

There was the risk of a stalemate, and so Caiaphas regained his grip on the situation. He questioned Jesus again, and did so unerringly, asking, perhaps even more solemnly, the same decisive question Annas had asked shortly before, in the secret interrogation we have read about in John and Luke: "I put you under oath before the living God, tell us if you are the Messiah, the Son of God." Jesus did not disappoint him, affirming with equal emphasis: "You have said so. . . . I tell you, from now on you will see the Son of Man seated at the right hand of Power and coming on the clouds of heaven." We do not know how Annas replied, in the first interrogation. But now, before the assembled council, Caiaphas played his part to the full. Perhaps he really was horrified by the blasphemy of the answer. He tore his clothes—this was a ritual gesture—to stress the enormity of what had just been uttered, and suggested the epilogue: "Why do we still need witnesses? You have now heard his blasphemy. What do you think?"

It was a foregone conclusion. Everyone present thought Jesus deserved death. They insulted him, spit at him, and hit him, together with the guards.

PILATE WAS WAITING. He would have been informed about the events of the night, and that the Jews were preparing to transfer the prisoner. The time had come for the governor to meet the man who had cast fear into the whole Sanhedrin of Jerusalem. Perhaps he was curious. Certainly he knew he would have to be cautious. In Bulgakov's brilliant imagining, he had woken with a terrible headache.

2

ROMAN JUDAEA AND THE WORK OF THE FIFTH PREFECT

1.

Pilate was in Judaea from the year 26. As was customary for men of his rank, he would have arrived in Caesarea by sea, season permitting, at the artificial port dedicated to Augustus—"the size of Piraeus," writes Josephus—and built by Herod the Great, who had refounded the city on the site of an old Phoenician settlement known as Straton's Tower. The ambitious sovereign had also given it the new name—again in honor of Augustus—and embellished it with splendid Roman Hellenistic monuments, of which some traces remain today.

Where Pilate came from we do not know. His life before the posting to Judaea is a blank for us: lost information. We do not even know his praenomen, though, as we shall see, it may have been Lucius or Titus. We can suppose his origins were Italian, as was still the case in those years for most functionaries of his standing. Epigraphs dating to the republican epoch attest to the existence of Pontii between Campania and Latium, with minor roles in local politics, but nothing authorizes us to think that any of them were ancestors of the governor. All we can say with certainty is that he belonged to the equestrian order; in the political organization of that age, the province of Judaea was always administered by equestrians.

Rome was, like many societies in antiquity, a community of orders and statuses more than of classes: patricians and plebeians; free men, slaves, and freedmen; equestrians and senators; peregrines, Latins, and Romans, and so forth. Naturally, differences in wealth also carried significant weight, but they were not the sole point of reference, nor on their own did they determine positions and hierarchies. Other ties, established by birth and tradition, came first. At the top of the imperial social system were two orders whose origins date back to the heart of the republican age: the equestrian and the senatorial, the latter constituting the nobility in the narrow sense. A somewhat rough analogy, which has caught on, identifies the first as a kind of bourgeoisie of speculators, traders, and wheeler-dealers, while the second consisted of a genuine aristocracy of land ownership and lineage—though such assimilations must be treated with caution. The two groups had been effectively at odds with each other for a long time, and the bitterness of the conflict was a key factor in the crumbling of republican institutions. One of Augustus's first objectives had therefore been to reestablish a certain harmony between them (already called *concordia ordinum* in Cicero's constitutional lexis), one capable of bringing political and social peace to the ruling elites, or at least of regulating its competitiveness. In the ensuing compromise, the nobility lost certain privileges but regained a sense of security.

An essential point in the search for this new equilibrium was the identification of a public career reserved specifically for equestrians, flanking the traditional one destined for senators, allowing members of both orders to aspire to positions of great responsibility. The steps in these paths—especially in that of the equestrians—only began to crystallize over the course of time, thanks to the weight of precedent; it was not until the age of Hadrian, in the heart of the second century, that the progression envisaged for equestrians became fixed in a stable and articulated form. In the early decades of the first century, it was still distinguished by a certain fluidity, with much being decided according to the circumstances of the moment; and often the rank of a position depended more on the person holding it than the level of the post itself.

The career of the equestrian Pontius Pilate unfolded entirely within this framework—not yet clearly defined, but marked by a newfound unity in the government of the empire.

AUGUSTUS ALSO TURNED HIS ATTENTION to another essential task: he reorganized the administration of the provinces, which had developed up to then in a fragmentary and improvised way in response to the dizzying pressure of conquest. This work would continue for a long time, well beyond his rule. The high imperial officials and jurists contributed to it with great commitment during the first and second century, and the effort would carry on till the Severan age. The result was the construction of a carefully structured and rigorous administrative system, for Italy and the provinces, under the influence of a legal culture whose formal elaboration—though conceived at first for private law alone—proved to be an extraordinarily powerful and effective tool for managing powers, peoples, and territories. But at the time of our story, in the age of Tiberius, this undertaking—which we might call the juridicalization of the empire's political and institutional framework—was at its beginning, and care must be taken not to project onto the reality of that epoch outcomes and balances that would only be attained much later.

One fixed point, introduced at once, was the distinction between imperial and senatorial provinces ("Augustus divided the whole territory [of the empire] into two parts, and assigned one to himself and the other to the people," as Strabo, a first-century geographer and ethnographer, effectively put it). The governors of the latter were chosen by the senate from within its own order, among ex-consuls or ex-praetors. For the former (which almost always held a greater concentration of large military units), appointments were made directly by the emperor, as the expression of a wholly peculiar relationship—progressively defined in administrative praxis and legal reflection—with "his" provinces. The emperor's choice might fall on a man of senatorial rank, as happened for provinces like Syria, or, for territories which, like Judaea, had marked characteristics of personal domains—in that they had formerly belonged to vassal sovereigns, to whom the *princeps* in person seemed to be the immediate successor—on members of the equestrian order.

Of the twelve governors of equestrian rank who succeeded one another in Caesarea during the Julio-Claudian age, Pilate was the fifth: before him there had been Coponius, from the years 6 to 9; Marcus Ambibulus, between 9 and (around) 12; Annius Rufus, from 12 to 15; and Valerius Gratus between 15 and 26, as Josephus diligently records.

For none of them, unfortunately, are we able to reconstruct functions and tasks performed before their posting to the province; not even in this indirect way, then, can we dispel the darkness surrounding Pilate. We do know, however, that in this age the start of an equestrian career was still almost invariably military, and there is no reason to doubt this was the case for our governor as well, maybe as prefect of an *ala* (and before that, perhaps, prefect of a cohort or military tribune) in some legion stationed outside Italy. This did not necessarily make him a man of arms in the professional sense—he might have cultivated other vocations and talents—but it gave him experience of military matters.

Can it be conjectured that, in performing his duties, he had occasion to meet Tiberius personally, or at least came into contact with his close circle of aides and field officers—of his high command—and was pointed out by them to the future emperor? Regrettably, we have no conclusive proof of this. Tiberius, who succeeded Augustus in 14, had been an excellent military commander, intuitive and prudent, with strategic vision and tactical flair. But his feats—in Armenia, Germany, and Illyria—coincide only marginally (because too early) with the dates of Pilate's presumed army service. His campaigns, in fact, are concentrated between 25 and 6 BC and between 4 and 12. We would have to think that in the course of his final ones—maybe in Germany between 9 and 12—he noted a young Pilate, officer in one of his legions, and that this carried some weight later on, when he became emperor, leading, perhaps after a further test in a lower-profile post, to the appointment in Judaea. It is hypothetical, but not implausible. In this case, Pilate would have been around forty years old when he arrived in Caesarea.

A relationship must have been established in some way or other, if not with Tiberius in person, at least with someone very close to him: the governorship of a province was not obtained, and then kept for so long (ten years was an unusual length of time, matched, in that post, only by his predecessor Gratus, also appointed by Tiberius just after becoming emperor) without a solid and direct link to the upper tiers of the empire.

If this is true, it may be possible to propose another reconstruction as well. When Pilate obtained the prefecture of Judaea, the principate of Tiberius was going through a crucial phase of change. Twelve years after his investiture, the emperor left Rome, accompanied by only a small group of friends, and established himself soon after, and for good, on Capri—which he had discovered thanks to Augustus, and had lain close to his heart ever since. The emperor had a reserved and difficult character, and was deeply attracted by isolation and darkness: already once before, in the height of maturity (at least according to the Roman idea of life: he was thirty-six), he had abandoned Rome, secluding himself for eight years on Rhodes, another small island he greatly loved. He had been sorely tried by a stormy and contorted relationship with Augustus, and later by the dramatic and premature death of his son Drusus, poisoned in 23, seemingly with the complicity of Drusus's wife, Livia Drusilla. The Julio-Claudians were truly a cursed family, overwhelmed to the point of self-annihilation by the boundless power that fell into their hands.

From Capri, Tiberius continued to attend to the management of the empire (he had an extraordinarily efficient communication service), and it is highly unlikely that he simply sank into the dissoluteness later attributed to him by Tacitus and Suetonius. But inevitably, he delegated some of his duties. The man he chose was Lucius Aelius Sejanus, another equestrian, and like Tiberius a man of darkness, prefect of the Praetorian Guard from 14 to 31.

It is possible—though this too remains a conjecture—that Pilate was chosen by Sejanus and not directly by Tiberius. There is insufficient evidence, however, to demonstrate that his posting was linked to an anti-Jewish strategy pursued by the prefect of the Praetorians around this time, and that he received a specific mandate to persecute Jews in their land of origin. Admittedly, in 19, a measure—possibly a senatusconsult (senatorial decree)—did order part of the capital's large Jewish community to leave Rome, together with several thousand followers, mostly freedmen: Tacitus mentions it briefly. But this was probably a decision associated with the repression of practices of worship deemed to be potentially dangerous, and with the protection of public morality; besides the Jews, the cult of Isis was also targeted. We can suppose, with some grounds, that Sejanus's policy was tinged by anti-Jewish attitudes, but it is much less likely that there was a protracted design of full-blown persecution. Philo seems to believe it, and his testimony should not be underestimated, but it is possible to detect a rise in this hostility only in Sejanus's last years of power. The episode of 19 left no lasting trace, and in the space of a few years the Jewish community was larger and more deep-rooted than before.

If Pilate is to be regarded as Sejanus's man, we would have to assume that the latter's death in October of the year 31, stripped of power and deftly eliminated by Tiberius (a kind of coup d'état in favor of himself), coincided with a difficult period for the governor, who would have suddenly found himself without his most important point of reference in the capital. If this was so, the crisis was overcome rapidly and without damage, given that Pilate remained in office another five years, until the end of 36—a sign that, irrespective of who put him there, Tiberius continued to trust him.

2.

Pilate had very wide powers. His title was that of the prefect of Judaea (*praefectus Iudeae*), though there are oscillations in the nomenclature attributed to this post by literary and epigraphic sources, which have long divided scholars; Tacitus, who calls Pilate "procurator" in a celebrated passage we shall look at presently, uses only—with an anachronism—the customary qualification from the time of the emperor Claudius onward, which was therefore in use when he was writing.

From a formal point of view, the *princeps* alone stood higher than Pilate in his province. Historians have advanced the possibility that the governor of Judaea was subordinate to that of nearby Syria—also a province controlled directly by the emperor, but much larger, where the most substantial forces in the whole Roman East were stationed, headed by a delegate of the emperor (*legatus Augusti*) of senatorial order and proconsular rank. In reality, it is improbable that there was a legally recognized hierarchical dependence between the two governors in this epoch, other, perhaps, than in a strictly military ambit. The ordinary running of Judaea was a matter for Pilate alone. That said, in the power relations taking shape within the Roman administration on the eastern checkerboard, the legate of Syria carried much more weight than the prefect of the small and almost unmilitarized Judaea. The latter would have regarded his important neighbor as a kind of senior colleague, to turn to in particular circumstances, and from whom he could expect, if not strict control, then at least attention and supervision. This would happen, as we will see, toward Pilate as well, who, during his decade in office, saw three governors succeed one another in Syria: L. Aelius Lamia, probably already in office at the time of Pilate's arrival and who remained there until 32, and therefore to the (most probable) year of Jesus's death; L. Pomponius Flaccus, until 35; and finally, from 35 to around 39, L. Vitellius.

Since the republican age, the Romans had defined as *imperium* the general power of command, military and civil, of their leading magistrates (consuls and praetors). According to a model charged more with ideological value than constitutional actuality, and which served to maintain for the new regime a continuity with the republican order, the *princeps* himself received it symbolically from the hands of the people gathered in assembly. Through a series of transitions and analogies, this same power was generally accorded to the governors of the provinces, within the spatial and temporal limits of their mandate. Some late testimony from Ulpian—a great jurist of the Severan age—assures us that this also held true (as it did, we can believe, from the outset) for the prefect of Egypt, of equestrian rank but invested by law with an *imperium* "similar to that of a proconsul."

Was this equally true for the other prefects? We do not know. Josephus, in the *Antiquities*, tells us that Coponius—the first governor of Roman Judaea—ruled the province "with full powers," and previously, in the *Wars*, that "he was also granted by Caesar the power to sentence to death." There is no reason to believe his successors experienced any restrictions in this regard. It is, however, by no means certain that, in Roman thinking, holding these posts was equivalent to being invested with *imperium*. But it did mean that the governors of this province possessed incisive powers—including that of putting a subject to death—modelled in some way on the *imperium* of the proconsuls and of the propraetors. This must have applied to Pilate as well.

Whatever the rank and formal qualification of command, for officials at that level the concrete content and the limits on the scope for intervention and coercion were always elastic, regulated more by practice than by rigid normative frameworks, especially at the beginning of the first century. Their duties usually concerned civil and criminal jurisdiction; fiscal affairs, that is, the right to impose and collect taxes in the name and for the benefit of Rome; and, finally, public order and the military defense of the province, to which end the governor was at the head of the troops stationed there.

For criminal repression in particular, one distinction was significant: that between provincial subjects without Roman citizenship, and Roman citizens. The existence of this dual regime was, at the time of our story, incontrovertible. When provincials were involved, justice—penal, above all—was managed much more in compliance with what must have appeared to the Romans as the goal of substantive equity—albeit always from the point of view of the conquerors—than in observance of a rigidly predetermined legal procedure. It must also be borne in mind that in this age nothing resembling a complete system of penal law, in the modern sense of the word, existed in Rome either, only a collection of statutory laws interpreted by forensic orators and by jurists. It was a question, then, of knowing how to dose almost boundless powers of decision, which included that of life and death, and was totally unrestricted from a narrowly legal point of view.

Limits did exist, of course, intended to prevent abuse, but they were solely and specifically political. Rome governed first and foremost through consensus, and, where possible, through integration, cultivating privileged alliances with the different local aristocracies: loyalty in exchange for legitimation of their own privileges.

This was true in Judaea, as Pilate knew very well. The equilibrium presupposed a moderate and—if we can put it like this—"pedagogic" use of the power of coercion. Behind him the governor had, and could not forget, the shining persuasiveness of a prestigious legal tradition without equal in other cultures. The "majesty" of the Roman people—we would say its recognized authority and its hegemonic capacity—did not rest merely on arms, but also on legal tradition, on *ius*: a word and a notion untranslatable in any other ancient language. "Brute force bereft of wisdom falls to ruin by its own weight," Horace had written shortly before—a view shared by the imperial elites. It was for this that Greek thinkers familiar with the ruling groups of the capital—from Polybius to Aelius Aristides—saw the Romans as the extraordinary inventors of a world order founded on reason and measure: every functionary at the head of a province had to live up to this expectation and this judgment. A similar pattern of thinking would long inspire the model of the ideal governor, constructed with able efficacy:

It is appropriate for a good governor who takes his duties seriously to see that the province under his control is kept quiet and peaceful. He will secure this without difficulty if he takes conscientious measures to make sure that the province is free from malefactors and that he hunts them out: he must therefore track down everywhere temple robbers, bandits, falsifiers and thieves, and punish each according to their crime, and also castigate those who harbor them, without whose help no outlaw can remain at large for long.

Ulpian—the writer here—was working at the beginning of the third century, but summed up, as he was wont to do, a well-established tradition. There is no reason to believe his precepts were not already valid at the time of Pilate.

Things were different if a provincial governor had to administer criminal justice with regard to a (non-military) Roman citizen resident in his territory. In this case, he had to take account of consolidated institutional guarantees—whose origins date back to the heart of republican history, and to the remote practice of appealing to the people—which protected every citizen, in Rome or in Italy, against a magistrate's abuse of his role.

In the decades of our tale, though, the Roman criminal trial was undergoing a profound change, linked in large part to the advent of Augustus's regime and those of his successors, and to the introduction of a new procedure, not bound by the republican magistracies but entrusted instead to officials of the *princeps*. This shift—made even more complicated by the fact that the new system did not replace the former one but, in line with a typically Roman habit, ran alongside and gradually emptied it of significance—makes the field extremely tangled for us, especially in relation to the Julio-Claudian age and to peripheral areas of the empire like Judaea. It is certain, however, that an accused citizen could demand to be tried in Rome and not in the province, and could even go so far as to request the intervention of the emperor himself.

Without a doubt, then, a governor such as Pilate, if he believed problems of public order were at stake, or if he deemed a law of the mother country to have been violated—not long earlier, for instance, Augustus had introduced an important measure relating precisely to the repression of violence—was fully authorized to act toward provincials using methods that were in his power to decide. If circumstances required, and above all if he was dealing with a person of low social standing (a discrimination applying also to Roman citizens living in Italy), he could proceed in a highly perfunctory manner, just as the *tresviri capitales*, the capital's police chiefs, did in Rome. We can thus safely say that, in this epoch, every problem concerning the repression of crime ended up being, in the empire's non-Italic territories, chiefly a problem of a political and not a legal nature: a question of measure and coherence in the discretionary use of coercive force.

3.

The Roman ruling groups had long been aware that the strength of the empire lay in its unequalled capacity to absorb different peoples, following a route that went from conquest to subjection and finally (when conditions were ripe) to assimilation.

The rules regulating that path for centuries were diverse, and would always be prudently combined with a further general principle, apparently at odds with the practice of integration but in reality concurrent with it: that of autonomy. Wherever possible— and above all, wherever there were cities—local communities should continue to abide by their own traditions and laws: *suis moribus legibusque suis uti,* in the pithy formulation used by the emperor Hadrian in a celebrated speech reported by Gellius, less than a century later.

According to an elementary but effective imperial anthropology of conquest and domination—already evident in the first century BC, in Cicero's time—it was also considered opportune to make distinctions on the basis of the cultural and organizational level of the peoples to be governed. To the west and north of Italy, subjection could mean nothing other than the Romanization and urbanization of sparsely populated "barbaric" territories. But to the east, in the vast Mediterranean spaces already traversed by the wave of Hellenization—language, emigration, political forms—and where there were far more ancient civilizations than the Roman one, with a dense network of urban settlements, much greater caution was required, and subjection and inclusion needed to take more complex routes. This was true for Greece, naturally, but also for Egypt, Syria, and the province of Asia. It was true for the territory governed by Pilate as well—as he was quite aware.

ROMAN JUDAEA WAS A VERY small region: about 160 kilometers from north to south, from Caesarea to Gaza, and 70 from east to west, between Gaza and the Dead Sea: smaller than Piedmont or Sicily, roughly the size of Connecticut. It comprised the territories of Judaea proper (including Jerusalem), of Idumea, and of Samaria (including Caesarea and Sebaste), but not of Perea and Galilee: that is, it did not take in the whole of Palestine, which itself barely covered twenty thousand square kilometers. Cramped spaces, not many cities, and far fewer than a million inhabitants: a land of small free farmers, with a high density of settlements taking the form of innumerable villages populated by peasants, shepherds, and fishermen; a limited landed aristocracy often associated with priestly functions; an economy more geared toward self-sufficiency and local markets than to large-scale trade over long distances— but already imbued with an almost incredible overload of religious memory and of the symbolic transfiguration of places and recollections, structured around the Bible and the Temple of Jerusalem, which continually weighed upon and marked the rhythm of daily life and its mental imprint. This, then, was Judaea in the time of Christ.

In this sharp contrast between the modesty of real contexts and the forces at play within them, and the almost incalculable power of a religious elaboration that transcended and annihilated them in a never sufficiently satisfied need for oneness and for the absolute—a single God and a single "chosen" people, in a direct and exclusive relationship with Him—a whole anthropology was taking shape and coming to light: a framework of thoughts, behaviors, and relations for which the existence of the Bible was at once cause and effect, presupposition and result. Perhaps the first person to have some perception of this in Roman imperial circles was Posidonius, a Greek philosopher of the first century BC, who was perfectly integrated into the ruling groups of the capital and keenly interested in ethnographic travels.

It was a gap, probably deriving from remote anxieties and profound collective traumas, between the poverty of history and the extraordinary richness of memory; or, if we wish, between the normality of real history and the exceptionality of history in thought—both imagined and remembered—with the latter called upon to redeem the meagerness of the former, mixing together, in a tumultuous and fascinating accumulation, theological structures and figmental chains of characters and events. The contradiction gave full expression to the political drama and the cultural power of ancient Israel, of the *éthnos tôn Ioudaíon*, with its surging impulse of identity and unarrestable theocratic vocation—at least from the Babylonian exile and from the Diaspora onward, insofar as we can grasp it today. Religious memory, which was inseparable from the political, moral, and intellectual history of the whole people—and indeed the only way the latter could take shape and recognize itself as such—thus became an all-pervading reality, on which everything depended. The story of Pilate and his encounter with Jesus was marked by this tension.

Upon his arrival in Caesarea, the new governor would certainly have had time to familiarize himself with a little Jewish history, at least the most recent, enough to perform his most important tasks: to ensure the social stability of the region and to oversee its administrative framework, especially from a fiscal point of view.

The Romans had entered into contact with Judaea at the beginning of the second century BC, after the victory over Antiochus III and the peace of Apamea, in 188 BC—the years in which the aristocratic ruling groups' quest for empire was acquiring the irreversible features of world dominion. In 161 BC came a full-scale treaty of friendship and alliance (the existence of which has been wrongly doubted), formally on an equal footing, which helped the Jews in revolt to move even more decisively out of the orbit of the Seleucid sovereigns and accelerated the definitive disintegration of their empire, just as the Romans had intended. The agreement was renewed many times between the second and first century BC, and accompanied the Hasmonean dynasty's long struggle for the full independence of Judaea. Thanks to its success, the country effectively managed to achieve complete political autonomy, though it became locked into an increasingly asymmetric relationship with Rome, which proclaimed itself the guarantor of Judaean liberty and was now unabashedly interested in establishing a powerful hegemony over the whole of the Hellenistic East.

In the meantime, the traditional theocratic and hierarchical organization of Jewish society was feeling the ever stronger impact of Greek-language cultural penetration—induced in particular by the Seleucids, who had also encouraged sizable foreign settlements—which had been absorbed in a relatively peaceful way in the previous century. The confrontation with Hellenism is undoubtedly the most tormented and complex aspect of Jewish history in this age: a theme, despite much important research, still to be explored in depth. Even though some strands and forces in Jewish society—and in Jerusalem itself—were in favor of giving new shape to the religiosity of Abraham and Moses, which had been crystallized by custom and observance, we can confidently say that the two worlds never meshed. The encounter was an almost totally missed occasion, even though it would leave many traces. The impact broke up and exhausted itself in a proliferation of hotbeds and causes for attrition—some ethnic as well—in which the possible Hellenistic reform of Judaic particularity came to be seen, and really was in the end, as an attempt to "abolish the Torah." The edict of Antiochus IV, who in 168 BC, pressed by the more extreme fringes of the Hellenizing movement, effectively prohibited the very practice of Judaism, prompted the start of the fight for liberation from the Seleucids, a clash in which the popular struggle to preserve traditional identity blended with the battle for religious restoration and for the primacy of the Jewish ethnos over the Greek element.

The cultural conflict that took place in this small peripheral setting—Hellenism and Hebraism, with the Roman power in the background: the triad which shaped the path of the West—was nonetheless a decisive contest. We cannot say what would have happened if the contact between Hellenism and that "alien wisdom" had produced different results, less conflictual and more syncretic: if Greek intellectuals had learnt Hebrew and Aramaic, and if Jewish religious culture had been more receptive to Hellenistic thought. Certainly, the course of the whole of the West would have been different, as too, without a doubt, would have been the relationship of Judaism with Christianity, which, by contrast, in its encounter with Greek culture produced—from Paul onward—inclusive, successful, and in some ways extraordinary outcomes. But that is another story.

Riven by disruptive pressures, the contrasts within Jewish society became even more acute in the early decades of the first century, and from then on would never heal. It was partly for this reason that the anti-Roman revolt of 66 turned into a bloody showdown between factions. Though the Hasmoneans had won back freedom for the Jews, even reconstituting in a single function regality and high priesthood—in other words, fully restoring the ancient theocracy—they were not able to defend it. Their policy ended up provoking further fractures within the priestly aristocracy and attracting further Roman attention. In 63 BC, grasping the opportunity offered by an internal dispute between Hyrcanus and Aristobulus, the last heirs of the dynasty, Pompey, who had already taken Syria, marched into Jerusalem and profaned the Temple by entering it as a foreigner. From then on, writes Josephus, "liberty [of Judaea] ends and subjection to the Romans begins."

Pompey did not, however, create a new province: he merely accentuated the asymmetry of the alliance, turning Judaea into a kind of protectorate—a solution that had long been employed in the flexible Roman imperial practice. He granted Hyrcanus II the title of ethnarch (not of king) and high priest, made his people tributary to Rome, and deprived Judaea of access to the sea by detaching the coastal strip; in the Psalms of Solomon the military conqueror is presented as an unconscious instrument of divine punishment for the sins of Hasmonean Israel, roundly condemned without reserve. A whole historic cycle, which had begun with resurgence, thus ended in complete disaster.

Pompey's setup did not last long. In 57 BC, Aulus Gabinius, proconsul of Syria, split Judaea into five distinct territories— "toparchies"—each under a local Sanhedrin, maintaining for Hyrcanus just the high priesthood. In fact, religious life remained unified in these years; the absence of significant urban centers and the fragmented agrarian landscape seemed to justify such an arrangement. But this did not survive either. In 47 BC, Julius Caesar reestablished the unity of Judaea, gave back control of the coast, reaffirmed the right of its people to live according to their religion and laws, and once again entrusted its government to Hyrcanus II (still as ethnarch), flanked by his advisor Antipater—a notable from Idumea viewed with great favor by the Romans, whom he in some way represented—but left it as a tributary of Rome. This was a point that remained fixed, even if the tax levies were a heavy burden for the Jews.

The events following the death of Caesar in 44 BC had repercussions in Judaea. Antipater died of poisoning the following year; Hyrcanus—once a prisoner of the Parthians, who had invaded the country—was removed from power after 40 BC (he would die in 30 BC). His son Herod (later called "the Great"), in exile in Rome, was proclaimed king by the Roman senate, and in 37, helped by Mark Antony's troops, recaptured Jerusalem and Judaea, which he maintained, as a vassal of the Romans, until his death in 4 BC.

I believe that Herod should be considered as continuing, with other means and strategies, the Hellenizing design of the Seleucids, realistically accepting that the Jewish religion was unreformable. With perceptive insight, he tried to separate the largely Pharisaic-inspired popular religious sentiment—presenting himself as its defender and protector—from the destiny of the priestly aristocracy, whom he consistently opposed with cold determination: in 37 BC, just after his return from exile, he put to death forty-five members of the Sanhedrin, almost all Sadducees, and confiscated their land and goods. In this perspective, his decision not to assume the role of high priest (he was not a Jew—though he tried to pass for one—and so was not eligible), while arrogating to himself the right to choose who should be and to limit the powers of the Sanhedrin, was seen as a gesture of respect toward the traditions and sensibility of the Jewish popular masses. At the same time, it gave him a free hand to strongly secularize political structures and public life, in line with the aspirations of the Greek-speaking pagan minorities. His programs of accelerated urbanization—in Caesarea and Sebaste—and public works, including the enlargement and embellishment of the Temple in Jerusalem and the reconstruction of the fortress of Masada, in southeast Judaea, were typical of a Hellenistic regality: they met the needs of the urban proletariat, and favored a charismatic relationship between sovereign and people at the expense of the aristocracy.

This was the most profound reform which, from within Judaea itself and not by way of foreign imposition, had been attempted since the Babylonian exile: a partial Hellenization, based on the separation between regality and religious tradition—respecting the latter, but implanting all around a totally renewed political (and in part social) fabric. And alongside it was an absolute loyalty to the Romans and to Augustus, with respect to whom Herod saw himself as a kind of agent. He was careful always not to disturb imperial interests and expectations in the slightest, especially in his fiscal reforms, in the convinced perception that Judaea was now an integral part of a system of world dominion that it would be unthinkable to oppose.

But even Herod's path proved impracticable, and did not outlive him. When he died, Augustus decided to confirm his testament, which divided the kingdom between his sons: Philip and Herod Antipas received about a quarter each (Antipas got Galilee and Peraea), while the remaining half, including Judaea, was given to Archelaus, who soon appeared to the Romans to be totally inadequate—in fact, none of the heirs lived up to their father at all. The contrasts that Herod had ably avoided during his reign flared up again, and Augustus, in AD 6, was forced to depose Archelaus and send him into exile. The priestly aristocracy, which had worked to oust him, calculated that, to restore at least part of its power, direct imperial control was the preferable solution: better to have a foreign governor than another uncontrollable king. Thus Rome—in the light of an evident crisis among supporters of the Herodian dynasty and the absence of a reliable leader—decided to set up the new province, in the order of which Augustus (and his prefects) figured as the immediate successors of Herod, assuming all his prerogatives.

4.

In Pilate's years religious differences continued to define the whole of Jewish society, as would happen much later in some ages and countries of Christian Europe (in France, for instance, or England between the sixteenth and seventeenth centuries). The distinctions produced a multifaceted and fragmented microcosm, shot through with continual tensions: not just between pagans and Jews, but within the Hebraic world itself. According to Josephus, who touched on this theme both in the *Wars* and the *Antiquities,* the Jews of the first century were divided into three "philosophical" schools: the Sadducees, the Pharisees, and the Essenes.

In reality these were not philosophies, as Josephus called them to make himself understood by his Graeco-Roman readers, but styles of life determining collective behaviors, political ties, and power relations—in a word, modes of social organization. His description nonetheless functions as an invaluable X-ray, enabling us to approach that universe.

The Sadducees—who perhaps did not believe in the immortality of the soul (a controversial point, unconfirmed by archaeological finds from their tombs)—considered as binding only what was transmitted in the Torah and lent no credence to the oral tradition. They had, according to Josephus, a harsh and aloof manner, and formed, as far as we know, a fairly small minority of the population, though they included the large aristocratic families that administered the Temple, from among which the high priest was chosen. The Sadducees were the most favorable to active collaboration with the Romans, had been perhaps the least unreceptive to Hellenistic influences, and were probably the most lukewarm in sustaining the exceptionalism of their religion. As a result, they were the first victims of the reckoning within Judaism after the insurrection of 66: their group was completely swept away, erased also from the memories of the later Jewish tradition. But in Pilate's time they had considerable power (gradually reacquired after the years of Herod), and were essential to the Roman system for controlling and building consensus in the territory and society of Palestine.

The Pharisees (Josephus considered himself one), on the other hand, enjoyed an extensive and certainly a majority following among the masses, in Jerusalem and in the villages. In the Gospels they come across as shortsighted and inflexible formalists, more concerned with the scrupulous observance of ritual than with the moral core of religious prescriptions. "Now you Pharisees clean the outside of the cup and of the dish, but inside you are full of greed and wickedness," writes Luke. But there is considerable exaggeration in this picture, which served to highlight by contrast the disruptive aspect of Jesus's thought: an ethical substantialism the likes of which had never been seen before. In the Pharisees' doctrine—which in many respects represented the common-sense view of the Jews in the period of Roman domination—the Torah was nothing other than a part of the Law of Yahweh, which had to be completed with study and scrupulous respect of the oral tradition, built up in layers from the pre-exile prophets through to contemporary rabbinic teaching. Rooted within this shared bedrock were other, and different, orientations, as is to be expected in such an ideologically reactive environment for a grouping whose ranks were so broad and varied: from the humblest social strata through to the "scribes" who interpreted the Torah, and members (however much a minority) of the aristocracy itself. In the age of Pilate, the Pharisees expressed in general an accentuated anti-Roman feeling with strong connotations of "national" identity, and were not insensible to the myriad of revanchist impulses that emerged at every opportunity.

Much less influential were the Essenes, a small circle of devotees who bore witness to their faith through study and a strict communal life. In the *Wars* (but not the *Antiquities*) Josephus wrote about them at length and in positive terms: "They turn aside from pleasures as an evil, and regard self-control and not succumbing to the passions as a virtue. . . . They despise riches, and their sharing of goods is admirable." Asceticism and a pure lifestyle—together with a prohibition against bearing arms—did not prevent the Essenes from being strongly hostile toward the Romans, nor from being very much to the fore in the revolt of 66. It is controversial whether the Qumran sect, which chose self-exile in a desert location in Judaea near the Dead Sea, was part of this movement, but the destruction of the settlement by imperial troops in 68 makes it evident that some connection must have existed between the two currents.

JUDAEA HAD ALWAYS BEEN A LAND of preachers and prophets, and it continued to be, all the more so, in the time of Pilate. The shared certainty of a privileged relationship with God brought with it a multiplication of those seeking to interpret and to announce His will. From the second century BC onward—coinciding with the most bitterly divisive phase of Seleucid domination—this prophetic vocation had begun to acquire increasingly strong apocalyptic tones and accents. The composition of the book of Daniel can be regarded as the turning point in this respect: defined as "a literature of combat," it imagined as imminent a catastrophic end of time coinciding with the final judgment of God, and was meant to comfort those fighting against foreign oppression: Seleucid or Roman. Eschatology and politics came together once again: the extreme redeeming of identity now overlapped, for the people of Israel, with the definitive and tragic completion of the history of humanity. The prospect of the apocalypse favored the flowering of messianism, which also seemed to be grounded in an obscure pronouncement by Daniel alluding to the imminent coming of the "Son of Man."

This militant theology contributed to the feverish mental climate in Judaea at the beginning of the first century. It fueled to no small degree what Josephus prudently—and with some hypocrisy—called Judaism's "fourth philosophy," which inspired the Zealots: a movement openly subversive to the Roman order, which it believed had to be fought immediately and without hesitation, even with guerrilla warfare and acts of political terrorism (Josephus speaks of "an ardent love of liberty, [the Zealots] being convinced that God alone is their guide and master"). It was an extreme and desperate way of making everything add up, even on what was fancied to be the brink of the apocalypse: real history and imagined history. As often happens in such cases, the Zealots' choice frequently rendered its adepts indistinguishable from simple outlaws, putting them into a gray area of rebellion and illegality that combined ordinary criminality, political insurrection, social revolt, and eschatological anxiety. Besides, banditry was a sore that had long afflicted the Palestine countryside, and the occupying imperial forces sought to repress it with the greatest severity.

The Roman governors tried, as far as they could and knew how—that is, not always in the best way—to manage this unstable and turbulent situation. Their imperial culture had not prepared them for unraveling problems so specific, delicate, and, we might say, unique: no other subjected population had produced anything like the Bible. In their efforts to "normalize" the province, they turned to the model most familiar to them: the formation of alliances with those segments of the local aristocracy prone to compromise, in this case the Sadducees and what remained of the Herodians—the least intransigent religious group and a Hellenizing secular circle—following the usual trade-off between the guaranteed preservation of privileges and pro-Roman collaboration.

The Roman prefects had inherited from Herod the power to appoint the high priest, while respecting the requirements demanded of such a figure by tradition—a right which Pilate would never exercise, as he decided to confirm Caiaphas (who had been nominated by Valerius Gratus) for all the years of his mandate. The imperial investiture put the chosen one in a rather particular position. He was the supreme representative of Jewish identity—religious and political, in a highly theocratic culture—but also the fiduciary of the occupying power. It was an intrinsically ambiguous role that left the high priest constantly exposed on both fronts: to the risk of popular discredit if he adopted an overly remissive or subaltern attitude toward the Romans, possibly to the advantage of a more charismatic and less compromised voice of popular emotiveness, and, at the same time, to the danger of compromising his relationship with the Roman authorities in the event of excessively autonomous or even irredentist behavior.

His powers—and therefore Caiaphas's—basically amounted to what the Romans permitted him. Certainly he had complete jurisdiction on religious affairs, excepting, however, the right to pass a death sentence (a disputed point, but I believe this is most likely); full control of the running, including the financial affairs, of the Temple, which was a kind of autonomous micro city-state in the ambit of the government of Jerusalem and even had its own police force—the one we saw in action during the arrest of Jesus; and, finally, certain administrative duties covering the whole of Judaea.

Functioning quite regularly alongside the high priest was the Sanhedrin of Jerusalem (this too is controversial, but I believe more radical suggestions that it was abolished in the imperial age can be ruled out due to a lack of any real motive), which was accepted by the Romans as the most important collegial organism of local self-government, in line with a model tested many times in Greece and the East. It was made up of former high priests (the one in office presided over it), some of the Temple priests, other members of the aristocracy (the "elders"), and the "scribes," learned interpreters of the Torah and of rabbinic tradition. The majority of the council was almost certainly Pharisee—in this it reflected popular if not exactly "democratic" demands—and the Sadducees heading it, insofar as they were high priests or influential former ones, had to take account of this far from easy equilibrium. The assembly's functions were uncertain at the time of Pilate: we can presume that it served as a court for religious matters, and perhaps also for some ordinary crimes, and that it had a number of general administrative competences over the whole of Judaea. But there were no precise boundaries, far less guarantees. Everything was once again referred to the Romans, who tended not to intervene unless imperial interests—political or fiscal—were affected, or acts were committed that seemed to violate Roman statutory laws.

5.

The governors usually resided in Caesarea, in a sumptuous marble palace built by Herod. Jerusalem remained the heart of the country's life, but all the administrative activity relating to the Roman presence took place in the coastal city, and the bulk of the troops stationed in the province were here too. Unlikely to have exceeded thirty thousand inhabitants, it was, like Sebaste, mainly pagan, had the appearance, very familiar to the Romans, of a Greek urban center, and (as we have said) possessed a large port—all of which were appreciable advantages from the imperial point of view.

So it was for Pilate as well. And now, thanks to a fortunate epigraphic find, we have an incontrovertible trace of his long presence in Caesarea. Excavations conducted between 1959 and 1964 by an Italian archaeological mission on the site of the ancient theater—a monument mentioned by Josephus as an example of the magnificence of the city—uncovered an inscription bearing the words: ". . . S TIBERIÉUM / . . . NTIUS PÌLATUS / . . . ECTUS IUDAE[A]E / . . . É . . ."

Four lines, on the front of a damaged block of limestone measuring 82 centimeters by 68: probably, in origin, an architectural fixture set in the wall of a tower, then used again (a habitual practice, and perhaps in this case not even the first reuse) as a step of a staircase in one of the reconstructions of the city theater dating to the fourth century. Here then, before us, is that name, legible in writing that goes directly back to his time: possibly the most famous epigraph of the whole Roman world.

Since its publication in 1961, there has been unabated discussion among scholars about the original location of the inscription, and how to integrate it so as to give full sense to the words and letters we are able to identify.

The epigraph evidently served to dedicate a building to Tiberius. Emerging from it is a glimpse of the prefect's government and administrative activities: Pilate paying tribute to his emperor. In the second line, without a doubt, is the name of the man making the dedication: Pontius Pilate. The remaining space on the left is not big, and suggests that the inevitable indication of the praenomen we do not know—abbreviated as usual to just one letter—must have been a T or an L, but not, for example, an M; for this reason, names like Lucius or Titus have been supposed. The title on the third line, again referring to the dedicator, is equally certain: "prefect of Judaea." The "Tiberieum" on the first line is more difficult to pin down. What does it refer to exactly? A temple for the imperial cult? A library? A portico? An unspecified building, but given the name of Tiberius?

One recent hypothesis seems to me particularly elegant and reasonably convincing: a fine example of the combined use of historical and archaeological documents. According to this reconstruction, the word, which was never used elsewhere (as far as we know), refers to a tower-lighthouse situated at the mouth of the port, similar and contiguous to—though perhaps more modest than—the one called the Druseum, mentioned by Josephus and named in honor of Drusus, Tiberius's prematurely deceased brother: two towers for two brothers—one dead, the other the emperor. The theater where the stone was reused and ultimately found was not far, as Josephus tells us, from the port and the line of the towers, which makes the hypothesis very plausible. Pilate, then, would not have built the monument (Herod did that), but simply renovated and dedicated it to the emperor: the "E" of the last line could therefore be completed as *refecit* ("remade"), while the solitary S on the first line might be part of the word *nautis* ("to sailors," who would clearly have benefited from the tower; like its bigger twin, it served as a refuge for them).

Whatever its exact meaning, that semi-erased inscription on a stone worn by time and use is the strongest of proofs—punctiform but irresistible in its uniqueness—that a prefect of Judaea named Pontius Pilate really was there in those years, just as the Gospels say and as Josephus and Philo of Alexandria recount: doing his job.

HOW DID PILATE GOVERN JUDAEA? We have a judgment of his administration—the only one of his actions and conduct as a whole—by Philo, the Jewish intellectual of the Diaspora and the head of the Jewish community in Alexandria. It is a starkly negative view: a "man of inflexible, stubborn disposition," with a "boundless and savage cruelty," "contemptuous and irascible,"

whose mandate was marked by "corruption, violence, robbery, torture, abuse, frequent executions without trial." In short, an unappealable sentence.

Philo wrote this in 41, at the beginning of Claudius's rule, in a partly autobiographical work entitled *Legatio ad Gaium* ("Embassy to Gaius Caligula"). It combines, not without some originality and some contradiction, Jewish orthodoxy, loyalism toward the Romans, and Hellenistic philosophical influences, above all Stoic. His harsh judgment was made in reference to an episode in Pilate's governorship that we will come to later, because it probably concerns the final period of the prefect's stay in Judaea, though actually the negative portrait is not precisely connected to the dynamic of the events he relates.

The judgment is widely believed to be unreliable. More than a real person, it depicts the type of the bad governor—as it had been crystallizing at least since the time of Cicero—made to correspond to the real Pilate merely on the basis of a theological prejudice. The words employed are likewise stereotypes: they do not delineate a character, but evoke a model, which, for the author, fits Pilate; no even barely determined circumstance emerges from the generality of the invective. Yet we should not be in a hurry to set it aside—because, despite everything, its partiality ends up revealing something more important.

Let's follow Philo's construction. He starts from an assumption that supports all his writing: anyone who does not respect, or who profanes, Jewish religiosity is wicked, capable of any crime, and sooner or later will merit divine castigation. Pilate is an example of this evil attitude, hence, in the end, his fall into disgrace and punishment; and thus he must, necessarily, have been a terrible governor, corrupt and cruel like all bad governors. The deduction is undemonstrated, as far as we can tell; from both the Gospels and Josephus a quite different figure emerges.

But was the presupposition ungrounded? In other words, what reason would Philo have had to attribute to Pilate the mask of the unworthy governor, in order to shroud his profile in a dark cloud of misdeeds? Evidently just one, but decisive: knowledge of Pilate's clearly hostile attitude to the Jewish religion. This premise was, for Philo, enough to transform him into a black-hearted and iniquitous functionary; obviously we cannot follow Philo in this judgment. But this does not mean that the point of departure was unfounded as well. Would he have included Pilate without hesitation in the list of the evil if the prefect's attitude toward Judaism had been notoriously tolerant and benevolent? We have no motive to think so. The flimsiness of the portrait betrays the much more solid foundation of the reason that prompted its invention. It is a fake, but built upon a truth.

Nothing confirms that Pilate committed the atrocities ascribed to him by Philo; and indeed, as we shall see, there are even some positive reasons for ruling it out. But it seems certain that he did not understand Judaic religiosity, that feverish and incomprehensible (to him) intertwining of theology and politics; nor did he have any sympathy for its ceremonies, its prescriptions, its prohibitions. It is possible, what's more, that this nonacceptance might have been compounded by a sharp-edged personality, inclined to mistrust and harshness. We can believe that this view of the governor's character and narrow-mindedness must have already been widely shared among his contemporaries, and that Philo took a common judgment as the starting point for his accusations. It was an act of defamation he could permit himself. Claudius was now in the emperor's seat, and the Jewish communities—in Rome and in Alexandria—were among many that could finally breathe a sigh of relief.

6.

The first episode that can be reconstructed about Pilate's activity in Judaea we owe to Josephus, who relates it both in the *Wars* and, in a rewritten but basically similar form, in the *Antiquities*.

The governor must have taken up his post not long before: the whole account suggests it. Grasping the opportunity of a routine troop movement—a unit, perhaps a cohort of infantry, moving from Caesarea to take up quarters in Jerusalem—Pilate ordered his soldiers to march into the city at night, carrying, as established by the Roman protocol for such occasions, their standards with a portrait of the emperor. This was a violation of Jewish law, which, in compliance with an extremely rigid aniconism, prohibited the display of any image ("You shall not make for yourself an idol, whether in the form of anything that is in heaven above, or that is on the earth beneath"). It is debatable whether this applied to non-Jews as well. But evidently the accepted interpretation was that exhibiting images in Jerusalem amounted to profanation.

The prefect knew of the ban perfectly well, just as he knew that none of his predecessors had infringed it, out of respect for

Judaic tradition. His choice was evidently deliberate, made with forethought. It was not a gratuitous provocation—an arrogant stunt—but a studied gesture. Pilate was gauging the capacity of popular reaction, and at the same time trying to get an idea of how far he could go in imposing on the territory—right inside Jerusalem and a stone's throw from the Temple (the soldiers would undoubtedly have gone to the Antonia Fortress)—the tangible signs of Roman sovereignty.

It was, in short, an initial test of the relations of force. The strategy was clear: Pilate was venturing beyond the invisible line fixed by earlier governors in order to attain a more advantageous equilibrium, to circumscribe Jewish religiosity in the face of imperial majesty. But he acted with a certain circumspection, and great caution. Not by chance, he had the troops enter the city unexpectedly and at night, as Josephus does not fail to emphasize, seeking to present the inhabitants with a fait accompli.

The plan does not work. At daybreak, the scandal explodes. The scene shifts now from Jerusalem to Caesarea, where "a multitude" of Jews assemble to plead with Pilate to remove the standards and the portraits. This is a wily and measured response to the governor's ploy, suggesting an orchestrated rather than a spontaneous move. The way to respond to the presence of the standards is not with a riot, with actions that might disturb public order or question Roman authority, provoking a reaction, but by asking the governor to reconsider his decision, and therefore acknowledging implicitly that only he has the right to do so. Did the Sanhedrin, and the high priest, play a part in such a careful management of the crisis? We do not know. Josephus—in the *Wars* as in the *Antiquities*—focuses exclusively on the relations between prefect and people, without alluding to the presence of others. The ideological significance of such a perspective is discernible, but its historical likelihood cannot be gauged. It is highly improbable that behind the demonstrators there was not some kind of direction: perhaps a difficult point of convergence between the priestly elite and popular movements of Pharisaic inspiration, an attempt by the Sadducee aristocracy to stitch together the fracture that had been open since the time of Herod.

The Jews who arrived from Jerusalem and the countryside remain in Caesarea for five days, gathered night and day around the governor's residence—without disturbances, but repeating their request in vain. Pilate is unyielding: to accept their complaint would be to offend the emperor.

Then the deadlock is broken. According to Josephus, on the sixth day Pilate goes to the stadium—a space given over to races, perhaps located near the hippodrome—and climbs onto a platform built specially for the occasion. The crowd of Jews follows him, to renew their plea. But Pilate is intent on forcing events, and has deployed a detachment of troops in combat gear, hidden from the crowd's sight behind the platform and perhaps some buildings. On a signal, three ranks of soldiers, swords drawn, surround the demonstrators, who are instructed to halt the protest immediately and to disperse. Otherwise, they will be run through.

The Jews do not yield. They do not resist with violence, but throw themselves face down on the ground, their bare necks stretched forward, ready to die as in a sacrifice rather than stand and watch their law being violated. It is a winning move. Pilate is taken aback. He is faced by an unexpected choice: back down or order a bloodbath. He decides to back down, and issues instructions that the portraits are to be removed from Jerusalem.

There is no reason to doubt the account, at least the essential dynamics of it. Josephus was normally well informed, and diligently used the documents available to him; for the years of Pilate, in particular, he had access to good sources, both oral and written. He might at most have altered a few details in order to emphasize his basic thesis, namely, that if the Jews were able to distinguish between religious conscience and submissiveness to the Romans, and the latter in turn knew how to show tolerance, provided their sovereignty was not cast into doubt, things would always work out for the best.

Pilate emerges as the loser in this first test. He himself had provoked the crisis, thinking he would score a point, and had to get out of it in the worst possible way—by capitulating. He would have realized, directly and dramatically, how religion was a crucial, all-consuming affair for that small people, and would have seen what a narrow line existed for them between ritual observance and pride of identity, between political irredentism and respect for the Torah. If there was someone in the background orienting if not actually directing the popular response, as we have conjectured—and such a figure would have likely come from the priestly groups—Pilate would have become even more aware of how difficult his governorship would be, and how ambiguous his supposed allies. In short, he would have realized what a complex contest it was that he had just begun with a false move.

Pilate did, however, demonstrate a capacity to change his mind at the right moment—and therefore his ability to evaluate and decide in an emergency, adapting flexibly to an evolving situation—rather than trying to win at all costs, even if that meant a bloody outcome (he was not, then, either stubborn or bloodthirsty, as Philo was to say of him). Undoubtedly, he was committed to his role as governor, and convinced he could do better than his predecessors; in a difficult environment and circumstances, he was learning his job.

7.

In the same narrative context, Josephus offers us a second rapid sequence of events—again in a double and almost identical version, in the *Antiquities* and the *Wars*—which fixes another episode in Pilate's activity in Judaea.

It is "some time after" the crisis over the standards: exactly when is not known, but if we place the first incident at the start of the prefect's mandate, between 26 and 27, and this one—sticking to Josephus's chronology—before the arrest of Jesus, we should be between 28 and 29–30.

Pilate had decided to have a large aqueduct built to supply water to Jerusalem. The archaeological identification of the route is controversial—and Josephus gives two different figures for its length—but the structure certainly extended southward, possibly starting from Ain Arrub. Herod, in his imposing building programs, had not taken such an initiative, and the city, which was packed with visitors during festivities, probably suffered from this lack. The construction of public works fitted perfectly into the duties of the good governor, and aqueducts were a strong point in the Roman model of urbanization.

To meet the cost of the undertaking, Pilate turned to the patrimony of the Temple: a significant resource, estimated at 2,000 talents in the age of Pompey. The treasure was kept inside the building, under the management of priest administrators, who, besides donations, received the proceeds of a levy of half a shekel that all male Jews aged twenty and over had to pay periodically, whether they were in Palestine or not (we know Augustus facilitated the raising of the tax and its regular shipment to Jerusalem). The wealth was used to fund sacrifices and maintain the Temple, but it could also be employed for the collective needs of the city.

That Pilate decided to draw on it for his aqueduct could not therefore have been cause for scandal: it was perfectly in keeping with tradition. Nor is it conceivable—and Josephus does not even hint at it—that he committed an act of violence in order to take possession of the money, or in some way violated the sacredness of the site where the treasure was held. At the most, he would have put pressure on the Sanhedrin and the high priest to contribute to his project. It is evident, then, that the whole operation was carried out with the consent—how enthusiastic we do not know—of the Temple administrators and of the high priest: an act of funding approved (or at least accepted) by the Jewish authorities for a work of public benefit.

Then complications began. Josephus is elusive on this point, and it is not clear exactly what happened. There may have been a growing sense among some segments of Jewish society that the money taken from the Temple was being wasted, or perhaps, for a reason we do not know, the very idea of building an aqueduct was unpopular. It is also possible that the priests themselves were against the project. The situation came to a head on a day when Pilate was in Jerusalem, probably to administer justice, and a crowd surrounded the court in uproar. It was not a sudden outburst of popular rage, but a demonstration prepared in advance: a kind of trap for the prefect. Pilate was not taken by surprise. Having learnt of the plan beforehand through informers, he had infiltrated among the protestors a detachment of soldiers, dressed in civilian clothes and equipped with clubs. Without using swords, they intervened in a robust and effective way—perhaps exceeding their orders, but quickly putting an end to the riot. Many died from the blows they received; others were trampled underfoot as people fled in terror.

This time Pilate's behavior appears frankly to have been impeccable, at least from the point of view of the good provincial governor; no Roman jurist—a Julian or an Ulpian—would have found anything reprehensible in it. The objective—the building of the aqueduct—was entirely worthy: it probably met a real need, and was in keeping with imperial urban planning policy. Taking the money from the Temple treasure was formally correct, in line also with Jewish rules. As things stood, the protest—certainly orchestrated, and of an undetermined size—could not be tolerated by the Romans. Pilate dealt with it well. He avoided an ostentatious deployment of troops in the city—never advisable in Jerusalem—and resorted to a different method, using the minimum of force and obtaining the maximum repressive efficacy. Admittedly, deaths occurred, some perhaps of passers-by (as the *Antiquities* seem to say); but public order had to be maintained. Without useless cruelty, and exercising the least force possible, yet without yielding an inch: it was a very measured response, all the more so if Pilate had glimpsed in the dynamic of the events the shadow of a trap, and some ambiguity on the part of the priests. The empire was not exactly a democracy.

Josephus appears to have been fully aware of the situation, and, especially in the *Antiquities,* I believe he places the two episodes, of the standards and the aqueduct, next to each other to show how the different outcomes—successful for the demonstrators in the first case, bloody and painful in the second—depended on the different attitudes of the Jewish crowd: firm in making its case but peaceful and respectful toward the Roman authorities in Caesarea, pointlessly violent and unruly in Jerusalem. It was possible to coexist with the Romans—this is Josephus's thesis—without being forced to disavow one's faith, providing care was taken to remain within the bounds of imperial legality, which Pilate, while certainly mistrustful, and distant from Judaic religiosity, seemed to interpret in an acceptable and not overly ill-disposed manner.

8.

After these brief accounts, in the *Antiquities* (but not the *Wars*) Josephus quickly mentions the death of Jesus, and for a short moment his writing intersects with that of the Gospel authors. The text has attracted a cluster of suspicions, according to which it should be attributed to a later interpolation. While what we read today certainly contains additions made by a later Christian hand, which probably also elided some sentences considered offensive to the new religion, there are no reasons—if not ones stemming from prejudices relating in part to sixteenth-century criticism—to doubt the authenticity of the rest of the writing. Present in all the manuscripts, and perfectly in keeping with the style and lexis of the author, is a passage that reads more or less like this:

About this time [of the two episodes just recounted] there lived Jesus, a wise man. For he wrought surprising feats and was a teacher of such people that accept the truth gladly. He won over many Jews and many of the Greeks. He was called the Christ. When Pilate, upon hearing him accused by men of the highest standing amongst us, had condemned him to be crucified, those who had in the first place come to love him did not give up their affection. And the tribe of the Christians, so named after him, has still to this day not disappeared.

There is nothing in this that is not in the Gospels. But one detail attracts attention: "When Pilate, upon hearing him accused by men of the highest standing amongst us . . ." What we have here is a source, or several sources—the ones drawn on by Josephus—independent of the traditions associated with the writing of the Synoptics and of John, and whose accuracy there is no reason to doubt, that confirms an essential point: the arrest and condemnation of Jesus had an impulse from within the Jewish priestly elite, which Pilate had deemed it opportune to go along with, if not to encourage. The two authorities—the Roman and the Jewish—proceeded side by side.

In an even more concise passage, Tacitus also refers to Jesus and his death. He had not read Josephus, but might have shared his source, and he was certainly well informed about Judaean affairs, the Jews of the Diaspora, and Pilate's mandate. If the seventh book of the *Annals* had not been lost, we would have a clearer picture of his knowledge.

> The origin of that name [Christians] is Christ, who during the Principate of Tiberius had been put to death by the procurator Pontius Pilate. This execrable superstition, repressed for the moment, would however break out afresh, not only in Judaea, the origin of that ill, but also in Rome, where the most terrible and shameful things converge from all parts and are magnified and exalted.

Here too all suspicion of interpolation must be rejected: who would have thought to add the name of Jesus in such a violently anti-Christian context! Instead, we hear clearly the severe voice of the historian, the contempt underlying Roman imperial rationality—certain of its foundations and rightness—for the aberration of a dangerous sect that had emerged from the dark depths of Jewish history. Nothing else can be seen here—and it is already enough.

For Tacitus, Pilate was in the right, like the priests who had requested his decisive intervention. Around a century on from the event, the conflict—anthropological and not just cultural—manifested itself in all its violence. Two worlds really were clashing.

Going to Pilate, on foot and in chains, after a stormy and painful night, Jesus must have been aware of it.

3

GOD AND CAESAR

+

1.

Jesus arrived at the governor's palace in the early hours of the morning. It did not take long to get there: the distance from Caiaphas's house was short. We can imagine him exhausted and sorely tried: for the whole night he had suffered insults, threats, blows. He had been subjected to heavy questioning by Annas, Caiaphas, and the priests of the Sanhedrin. But he was entirely in control of himself, as would soon be seen, and extremely focused. He was accompanied by a squad of Temple guards—probably the one that had arrested him the previous evening—and the members of the Sanhedrin present at the nighttime meeting, perhaps with their servants: the most important priests, but, we can suppose (following Luke), elders and scribes as well. Caiaphas and Annas are not mentioned again, but everything suggests they could not have been far away, at least for part of the morning.

The most detailed version of what occurred next is in John, and we will follow him in particular. I do not believe—though some important historians sustain it—that this choice obliges us to ignore the voices of Matthew, Mark, and Luke. I am unconvinced by the radical alternative: either John or the Synoptics. Certainly, in some points the narratives are drastically incompatible, and in these cases I think John's version is preferable. But in other details, the information is superimposable, or at any rate not at odds: combining the texts enriches our perspective, and there seems no reason not to do so.

The prisoner was taken into the palace, which John calls the *praetorion*, the word usually used for the governor's residence. The people who had accompanied him—guards, priests, scribes, elders, and anyone else—remained outside, waiting. John says it was "to avoid ritual defilement and to be able to eat the Passover": it was Friday, and the feast would begin that same evening. Yet it is hard to find any trace in Hebraic teachings of a rule that would have been violated if the Jews had crossed the threshold of the building: there was no corpse under that roof, nor was it given over to the worship of false gods. Besides, even the impure could attend the Passover supper. Perhaps the Jews did not enter because they were kept out by Roman officers, who had received orders to that effect so the prefect could question the prisoner discreetly. Still, no one left, and a small crowd gathered outside the palace to await developments.

In the meantime, in a room prepared for the occasion— probably on the ground floor just inside, as can be deduced from the dynamic of subsequent events—Jesus, still in chains, was brought before Pilate.

As we have already said about the heated nocturnal meeting of Sanhedrin members, not even what would take place now was a trial in the modern, intrinsically formal and legal sense of the word. Nor was it a trial in the less strict meaning we attribute to the term when referring to Roman criminal repression—that is, a procedure conducted according to the "order" (*ordo*) of public laws voted in assemblies or regulated "outside of order" (*extra ordinem*) by the new praxis of the emperor's functionaries. Jesus was neither a Roman citizen nor a provincial notable who deserved respectful treatment. He was a preacher of humble origin, unable to invoke either status or rank, who had become extremely dangerous in the suspicious eyes of the priests of the Sanhedrin, and was possibly a subversive intent on undermining the established rule. A perfunctory hearing, albeit mindful of Roman legislation and practice, would suffice to ascertain his guilt, and would be followed (if appropriate) by punishment, which might also be capital, imposed on the basis of the coercive powers delegated directly to the governor by the emperor. His incrimination might become a political issue, but certainly it was not a problem of statutory regulations and far less of law.

Pilate evidently knew what the Jewish authorities had against Jesus, and for this reason had authorized his arrest. The priests judged him to be a serious danger, for themselves and perhaps also for the Romans, and the governor had gone along with them so far. This had been enough for a police operation, but, to bring the prisoner publicly before the prefect and obtain a condemnation, more specific charges were required, relating in some way to crimes punishable by Roman statutory laws. Accusing Jesus of an act of violence would have been impossible to justify, nor could he just be charged with a religious crime because that would not have fallen within the imperial jurisdiction. Only one feasible option was available to his persecutors: to accuse him of a crime against the majesty of the Roman people and their sovereignty over Judaea.

The governor wanted the accusation to be made public: this was a constant concern for him in the hours that followed. He intended to prevent the arrest and probable condemnation from seeming like Roman complicity in a Sadducee conspiracy, with the risk of a popular uprising in defense of Jesus and, in that case, of a possible double-cross on the part of the priests, who might even declare themselves extraneous to the punishment meted out to the prisoner. He feared a trap designed to damage him, in which he might first be used by the Sadducee priests to rid themselves of a dangerous adversary, and then be abandoned in the face of popular indignation. Perhaps he had good reason to be wary. So, before starting the interrogation, Pilate—cautious, professional, perhaps moderately curious—stepped outside the palace and addressed the Jews waiting there, so that the charge might be openly declared: "What accusation do you bring against this man?"

At first sight the answer is surprising: "If this man were not a criminal, we would not have handed him over to you"—a statement that may even have sounded disrespectful in relation to Pilate's question. But we should be careful in reading this dialogue, and the following ones reported by John. They make no pretense to being a transcript of everything that was said. And how could they have been? They are isolated sentences, kept afloat by the thread of memory, taken from a set of words and gestures likewise uttered and performed on that occasion which have sunk into oblivion, fragments saved only because they were deemed by the tradition that memorized them to be revelatory of a thought, an attitude, a trait, or of a turn in events.

The priests evidently pointed out to Pilate—in public, in the open space before his official residence, after having told him many times in secret—how dangerous they considered Jesus to be, and which crimes, religious and political, he had committed. In this act of accusation they probably once again confused— carried away by feeling but also because in their culture the two areas overlapped—religion and politics, public order and fear of God. Luke's account completes John's version well here: "We found this man perverting our people, forbidding us to pay taxes to the emperor, and saying that he himself is the Messiah, a king," the members of the Sanhedrin apparently responded. But the governor was still not satisfied: he needed absolute clarity, from a Roman point of view. He wanted to protect his back. And that is why, at a certain moment—perhaps in the face of some ambiguity by the priests, in order to force them right out into the open—he said, "Take him yourselves and judge him according to your law." It was the quintessence of the Roman method of government, marked by respect for the autonomy of its subjects: *katà tòn nómon humôn*; *secundum legem vestram*.

It was an astute move. The trap now threatened to close on the accusers, who would have found themselves, in broad daylight, with the Passover imminent, having to deal with the awkward presence of Jesus, while at all costs they wanted the prisoner to become a Roman problem, to be solved with a Roman conviction. And so, worked into a corner—we do not know in what argumentative context—the priests were obliged to counter by saying, "We are not permitted to put anyone to death." Because it was the accused's death—and that alone—which they sought.

Historians have long debated the nature of the ban invoked by the Jewish notables: if the limitation was permanent, imposed by Roman power on the community's courts (essentially the Sanhedrin)—as I am strongly inclined to believe—or if the impediment was temporary, associated with the imminence of the Passover; or, finally, if it should be tied in to a general prohibition laid down by Mosaic law ("You shall not murder"). The fact remains that, in those circumstances, only the Romans could pronounce a death sentence.

Pilate had achieved his goal, and scored a point in his favor. He had forced the priests to publicly admit that they wanted the prisoner dead, and had forced them to formulate, again quite manifestly, a charge acceptable to the Romans, namely, that Jesus had proclaimed himself King of the Jews—of the people of an imperial province!—thereby seriously and blatantly subverting public order, and committing a crime that in Rome would be punished in compliance with the *lex Iulia maiestatis*.

The first scene ends here. The prefect goes back into the palace, orders Jesus to be brought forward, and begins to interrogate him, making it clear in his question what charges must have been leveled by the priests: he was guilty of *crimen maiestatis*, subject to the death sentence in Rome, and probably also of sedition and incitement to evade the obligation to pay taxes.

"Are you the King of the Jews?" he asks the prisoner, a question reported in the Synoptics as well.

We do not know in what language Pilate and Jesus spoke. Possibly in Aramaic—the local idiom—if Pilate had learnt it in his years in Judaea. Perhaps, but less likely, in Greek, though there is no evidence Jesus knew this language, while Pilate undoubtedly did and would have used it regularly in Caesarea. We cannot exclude the presence of an interpreter, called from among the governor's staff. Anyway, we can presume the pair were never alone. With Pilate was his security detail, who held the accused in custody, and his assistants. What was said between them certainly had witnesses, and perhaps a rough record was kept.

2.

The prisoner responded. But before reflecting on his words, we must ask ourselves a question I consider to be essential—one which, however, is strangely overlooked. In facing up to such a dramatic ordeal, however long awaited and foreseen—the achievement of his mission could not but pass by way of that meeting— was Jesus pursuing a strategy that determined his behavior? Did he have any objectives? Or was he simply improvising, overcome by anxiety and exhaustion?

That apparently unequal colloquy was the culmination of his preaching and his testimony, the point of convergence into which flowed the driving forces that had given form and meaning to his existence. He knew that what happened in the next few hours would shape the image of himself consigned to the world and to history—forever, defining the ultimate value of his message. Everything was encapsulated in that single picture: two men facing each other—one in chains, the other in the unopposed fullness of his power. But neither man represented just himself. Both were there in the name of an other, of whose will they considered themselves interpreters and executors: Pilate, in the name of the emperor, the "master of the world," as was known to everyone; and Jesus, in the name of his Father, equally as certain as Pilate, though his was a solitary certainty, exposed to doubt and anguish. In the image that had formed in his thoughts, and in the vision he would transmit to Christian memory, it was not the accused and his judge who were talking in the Praetorium of Jerusalem, but God and Caesar.

This transfiguration of an almost routine inquiry into the founding act of an epoch dominates Jesus's mind in those hours; it determines his words and, as we shall see, ends up involving Pilate as well. Nothing the prisoner says is improvised; nothing is left to the emotion of the moment. There was a mission to complete, and therefore a design to be realized, which the Gospel writings convey to us.

Jesus had a strategy, and with it he set out to attain two results. The first we might describe as being of a political–theological nature: there was for him a path to conclude. The second was more personal—if we can put it like this—but even more important, and concerned his own destiny. In any case, he did not say even a word merely to defend himself. He had a task to finish.

"Do you ask this on your own, or did others tell you about

me?" replied the prisoner. It was a cautious answer, provisional for now. Pilate's question was strong and incisive: it contained a crucial word—*basileús,* "king"—and went directly to the heart of the issue. But Jesus wanted to clear away all ambiguity, to fully understand the meaning of what he was being asked: was this a deduction by the governor, or were the opinions of others being voiced? He knew quite well, after the night spent in their hands, what the priests thought of him, but he wanted to see what they had then said to Pilate, how they had translated into politics—into terms of Roman criminal repression—the religious charges leveled at him in the nighttime interrogation.

Pilate understands Jesus's intention perfectly, and surprisingly has no difficulty responding, albeit with a certain justified (at least from his point of view) haughtiness. Such indulgence was not customary in the circumstances. An accused such as the one before him—a subject of humble origins, over whom there hung a very serious charge advanced by the assembly of his community—was not in a position to ask questions, even less so to the governor in person. His place was to answer them, if necessary under torture. Yet Pilate is willing to engage with him in less crushing terms. It is possible he had already been struck by the prisoner's personality. All of Jesus's preaching testifies to an exceptional magnetism, and the prefect must have been able to judge—at a glance—who he had before him: he would not have remained long where he was otherwise.

The questioning thus turned—at least for the moment—into a real dialogue. And I believe it is precisely this exceptionality that caused it to be preserved in Christian memory.

"Am I perhaps a Jew? Your own people and the chief priests have handed you over to me. What have you done?" said Pilate.

This opening served to reestablish limits, even if in an unusual and almost colloquial manner. The governor was the emperor's representative, and did not concern himself with popular rumors, from which, moreover, he would have nothing to deduce. Rather than disdain for Jesus in that observation, expressed as a rhetorical and derisory question—"Am I perhaps a Jew?"—there was instead a sign of Pilate's total remoteness from the society and religion of the country he was governing, the same attitude that must have motivated Philo's dreadful opinion of him, and which also emerges—albeit reined in by prudence and flexibility—in the episode of the standards. For the Roman prefect—who would never have said with equal harshness, "Am I perhaps a Greek?"—the Jewish religious sensibility was an opaque and distant universe, with regard to which incomprehension was at once a form of self-protection and a way of reaffirming Roman superiority. We do not know if Pilate had read the Bible, or any part of it, in the Greek version that had long been circulating between Syria and Egypt, but if so he was certainly not grabbed by it.

Then the governor shows his cards: Jesus is there because others have handed him over, he says. The prisoner knows this, of course. But that obvious affirmation, on Pilate's lips—followed by the question concluding this segment of the dialogue—becomes much more than a pointless statement of fact. John perhaps recalls it for exactly this reason. It was a first important admission that the Roman authorities, until the moment of the interrogation, had no significant charge to level at the accused. Everything was still up in the air.

Despite the intense pressure he must have been put under in the previous days by Annas, Caiaphas, and their followers in the Sanhedrin, it is a still reluctant Pilate who reaffirms that the initiative for the arrest has not come from him. His words sound almost like a justification—a first declaration of his extraneousness.

Particularly striking is the formula which, according to John, the governor used: "your own people and the chief priests." There comes to mind here the ancient Roman clause for indicating the city community in its entirety—*senatus populusque*, "senate and people"—adapted to Judaea, with the chief priests in place of the senators. Pilate might well have uttered precisely those words. If he did, we would be in the presence of a consciously forced interpretation, revelatory of his state of mind. "Your own people," he apparently said (this is how we must translate *ethnos,* and not as "your own kind," in the sense of a simple stressing of the ethnic identity between accused and accusers; otherwise the hendiadys with the priests would not have made sense): yet in the whole train of events thus far the people had not appeared at all. Nothing had been seen comparable to the crowd that went to Caesarea to plead for the removal of the standards, nor the one, perhaps obscurely fomented, that had protested over the aqueduct. Only the priests had entered the arena, gathered around Annas and Caiaphas, and with them the majority of the Sanhedrin, who Pilate certainly knew had been summoned to an impromptu meeting in the night, and who were now waiting in front of the palace. Were they "the people"? That would be hard to sustain, even considering the Pharisee component of the council. We must therefore deduce that Pilate was saying "your own people" in full knowledge that the body was in reality a narrow oligarchic group and not a genuine popular assembly—the latter being, what's more, an institution the Romans did not encourage in the cities of their empire, and not just in Judaea, preferring entities with a more reassuring aristocratic connotation.

The prefect did, however, have his own good reasons for making such an improper reference: with his declaration he wanted once again to extricate the arrest from the shadow of a Sadducee plot and to make it appear—even to Jesus himself—to be justified by a popular consent he feared it did not have. This had been a concern, perhaps the most pressing one, from the start: that Roman power might become the unwitting instrument of a factional struggle, sought only by the priests, and perhaps not even by all of them.

"What have you done?" Pilate concludes, resuming the thread of the questioning. He does not now ask Jesus if he has proclaimed himself to be the King of the Jews. Instead he tries to broaden the scope of the inquiry, asking him in a more generic way about his actions and words as a whole. Rather than pressing the prisoner on a specific point—the crucial one of regality, which had clearly been emphasized by the priests—he is asking why the Jews have dragged him into his presence. It is a kind of step back—a fresh surprise. He wants to compare the priests' version with that of the accused. It is as if he were restarting the inquiry from scratch. The Sanhedrin's report evidently was not enough. There is nothing to prove that Pilate did not intend to take it into consideration. But

the longer he had the prisoner in front of him, the less he found it
to be sufficient.

3.

We are not sure how Jesus replied. In John's version there seems
to be a jump at this point. "Jesus answered," we read, but we realize immediately that what he says does not refer to Pilate's last
question ("What have you done?"); and we do not know if this
is because the prisoner does not answer the prefect directly, or
because (as I believe likely) the Johannine account breaks here,
picking up at a later stage of the dialogue.

When it resumes, we see Jesus returning to the question with
which the interrogation began, and which he had at first avoided
("Are you the King of the Jews?"). Now, after whatever Pilate said,
the moment seemed to have come to unravel the knot.

"My kingdom [é Basiléia e emé] is not from this world [tou kósmou toútou]. If my kingdom were from this world, my followers
would be fighting to keep me from being handed over to the Jews.
But as it is my kingdom is not from here," he replies. It is a statement that would have sounded astonishing to Pilate: certainly far
removed from what he might have expected, though not disso-
nant with Jesus's teachings until then.

The Jewish religion revolved around an essential core, which
was at once theological and political: the Covenant—conceived
as a true contract, alternative to the search for any other form of
power—between a single and solitary God-person and the people

of Israel, who thus became the "chosen" people. In this way a particular relationship was established between political community and religious order, or, as has been said, between power and salvation. Behind this conception was an extraordinarily rich and productive cultural nucleus: its formation—its archaeology—is not yet sufficiently clear, notwithstanding much recent and important research, but it should be considered the real driving force of what we have described as the imagined history of Israel, and therefore of the Bible writings.

In this context monotheism figures more as an acquisition than as an original element, but once established, it became capable of elaborating, unlike all the other early religions of the Mediterranean area, a demanding critical relationship between truth and falsehood—between true and false religion—and of developing the radically new idea of a God who, not being able to be "represented" (hence the radical aniconism), made himself directly a legislator. The principle of the "regality of God" thus replaced the strictly political regality, which ended up being completely subordinated, to the point of dissolution. God was to reign without mediation.

This process makes the Bible at once a book of theology and the foundation of the Judaic "national" identity. It was within such a nucleus—as its presupposition and its consequence—that the strongest features of Jewish religiosity were consolidated: the intransigence of its monotheism, its identity-related exclusiveness—with the consequent theological construction (potentially violent) of the political relationship between friend and enemy, between followers of truth and followers of falsehood—its uncontainable theocratic vocation ("God himself and He alone is the one who will rule over you"). It is no accident that the word "theocracy" was invented by Josephus to describe the peculiarity of his country's political tradition.

Modern historians have rightly stressed the intertwining, in the historic functioning of this cultural construct, between theology and politics: a theology which, while originally stemming from politics (all theological concepts were nothing but political forms dressed up), gradually took its place after having absorbed its features. Theology and politics thus welded into a single "machine": the "theopolitics" of the Jewish people, which permitted human power only in subaltern forms. Each of the terms produced effects on the other, transforming its meaning and importance: the sacralization of ethics and the theologization of the idea of justice were among the first consequences of this fusion and exchange. So, for the Jewish people, incessant and unsated theocratic aspiration was the result of a long journey.

Jesus intervenes forcefully with respect to this deep-rooted construct. He does not deny, but transforms it. His preaching would be incomprehensible outside the framework of Jewish culture, which he had completely absorbed, and of which he must be considered a direct projection. But he chooses to radically reform the patrimony of emotions and ideas he has received—not to erase it, but rather to elaborate in a new way the relationship between power and salvation which formed its pulsating heart, finally closing the gap separating the imagined and the real history of Israel, and trying to reconcile the past (only thought) with the present (harshly tangible) of his people. The Judaic tradition was dissolved into a different design: not more mature (evolutionism as a yardstick of judgment for Jewish-Christian religious history would be wholly inappropriate and unfounded), but certainly more flexible and potentially more inclusive. It represented change; let's not say progress.

JESUS CUTS FIRST OF ALL into the theological framework of monotheism, introducing from within the revolutionary presence of the Son—that is, of himself. This transforms the One into Father, dividing him into Two thanks to the presence of the Son— two Persons in One—according to a figure of excluding inclusion destined to mark, through innumerable elaborations ranging from the Christian–Hellenistic tradition to Hegel, the whole of Western thought. The God-person remains firmly in place—and this will be decisive—but is now split. And that is not all. Jesus also brings the Two into himself, doubling into Man and God by virtue of his dual human and divine nature. It is through him, and him alone—and thus by way of the Two—that God, the One, enters time and history.

This is a reform of incalculable import, which implants the tension of movement, of negation, of contradiction even—in a word, of historicity—into a place where, previously, in the monotheist tradition, it had been unthinkable to look: the unitary constitution of the divine. Monotheism is not cast into doubt—the Father and the Son have the same substance—but now it appears no longer blocked within itself, caged in a statically self-centered configuration. Inside it there is now diversity, variation, difference of attitude and disposition, and all of this precisely in relation to the human, because it is only with respect to the human that the Father divides into Two and generates the Son, whose dual nature is the seal of a new covenant of God with humankind.

The separation between Father and Son presupposes unity. The monotheistic principle remains intact, and exclusion—the Son separated from the Father—always has the capacity to include once again. But the play of alternatives multiplies possibilities and perspectives. It depicts God as intrinsically a dialectic God—and dialectic in function to the human. The covenant with God exalts the human, but also modifies the very form of God.

The new binary construction of monotheism is reflected in the bond between power and salvation, or, to put it differently, in the structure and functioning of the Jewish theological–political machine. (The concept of "political theology" is not modern, nor does it start with Spinoza, as is usually believed; it is Roman–Hellenistic, and was developed in a cultural environment between the second and first century BC, from the circle of the philosopher Aetius to the jurist Quintus Mucius Scaevola, and the erudite antiquarian Marcus Terentius Varro.) The Two that now fills heaven is matched by a specular scission on earth. The theocratic dogma breaks: the theological–political enframing produces the duplication of worlds (*kósmos* in the language of John) and of the powers that underpin them: in heaven and on earth. When Jesus says, "My kingdom is not from this world," he is drawing a boundary, not digging an unsurmountable abyss. If he were to do so, he would end in a blind alley, and Christianity with him. Instead, in the same way in which the Two excludes in order to include (and yet excludes), so the separation between the kingdoms—that of God and that of Caesar—divides in order to connect: and yet it divides.

It is true, as has been elegantly sustained, that the course of any political theology inspired by monotheism—particularly of a modern one, I would add—cannot do without either of these formulations: the excluding ("my kingdom is not from this world") and the inclusive ("God alone will rule over you"). But such an affirmation cannot make us forget that it is by reelaborating the first of the two—the theology of exclusion inaugurated by Jesus within his reformed monotheism—that the whole history of the West acquired the features and substance that we recognize in it. In this sense, Judaism and Christianity cannot be traced back to the same "Archimedean point," as has been written. The change introduced by Jesus, passed on to the evangelical memory, and then—not without lacerations and oscillations—to Christian thought, which would develop it from Paul to Tertullian, to Eusebius, to Augustine, through to medieval scholasticism and Lutheran reflection, had opened a passage—which, for simplicity, we can describe as a breach of secularization—through which the whole path of Europe (and America), together with the overall structure of the modern state and its entire ideological frame, would pass. This does not mean that Christianity represents "progress" with respect to ancient Judaism. It only indicates a different road in the relationship between politics and monotheistic religion: a trail which has been much trodden, and of which we are the direct heirs.

When Jesus says that his kingdom is not from this world he is literally overturning upon itself the tradition of Judaic theocracy. The power of God is no longer reflected without mediation in earthly power: this novelty called into question all the history recounted in the Bible, and the political content of the Covenant itself. It did not deny them, but required that they be looked at in a new light—the light of a God that was no longer to coincide with the God of armies and to take the place of the sovereign legislator.

In his answer, Jesus shows no hesitation in appropriating the word thrown at him as a terrible charge: "kingdom," *basileía*. Once again theology reveals its political matrix. The chief priests had not been totally wrong in ascribing that title to him. He really was the King of the Jews. But the Romans did not have anything to fear from this claim either, because the power in which his regality is grounded "is not from here" (*ouk éstin enteûthen*). Precisely because it is incommensurable compared to every earthly power, it has a different origin, and develops according to a design that looks at earthly things from a different and alternative point of view, and traces with respect to them a boundary that can never be forgotten.

The distinction involved the tie between power and violence: an essential point in the Jewish tradition. In Jesus's words there is no direct link between the power of God (in heaven) and the earthly use of violence to impose respect for it on earth; thus the path was opened for a first "depoliticization" of monotheism. "If my kingdom were from this world, my followers would be fighting," says Jesus. It is at once a strong reference to his dramatic condition—he has not been defended by anyone—and an affirmation of its partial and provisional nature. Though humiliated by earthly power, he continues to be king in that other kingdom. The majesty of God is not measured by the force of arms: Jesus is in chains, and yet this does not prevent him from presenting himself as the Son of the Omnipotent.

This concept, crucial for him, had already been expressed, albeit in a less clear-cut way, in a celebrated episode related in virtually identical terms in the Synoptics, but not present in John—a precedent that illuminates and clarifies the magnitude of his affirmation in front of Pilate. "Render to the emperor what is of the emperor, and to God what is of God," Jesus had replied, after being shown a coin with Caesar's image on it, to a question about whether taxes should be paid to the Romans or not, put by Herodians, Pharisees, but perhaps also spies infiltrated from Jerusalem, who were laying a trap for him. The sense of the sentence seems to coincide exactly with what he says about the two kingdoms. In reality it clarifies its meaning, because a hierarchy is fixed. It should in fact be interpreted in a less conciliatory fashion than is usually thought. Jesus was not simply stating that imperial taxes had to be paid, on the basis of a straightforward distinction between what belonged to Caesar and what to God. His was an invitation to give up to Caesar, to abandon as a useless burden, what seemed to belong to him—money, with his portrait upon it—in favor of a more complete devotion to the things of God, that is, to inner human life and its salvation. It is almost as if he had exclaimed, "abandon to Caesar," giving to that imperative, which recurs in all three Synoptics, the pressing significance of a call for a radical renunciation and a brusque casting off—a reading proposed long ago.

The kingdoms—that of God and that of Caesar—are not on the same plane; there is no symmetry. They do not share equal dignity, and the relationship between them remains intrinsically problematic. What is of Caesar can be discarded without damage and does not cast doubt on salvation. What is of God requires total dedication. The dominating existence of the first realm wedges itself into the second, reducing and relativizing its value and horizons, even when the latter seems to be crushingly victorious. Each of us is always suspended between the two—and here the theme of scission returns: of the Father, of the Son, of the human—and must choose: for humans, the autonomy of the two worlds on the plane of history is at once the guarantee of liberty and the condition of a continual laceration.

An uninterrupted field of interferences connects the two planes. In the decisive one, God has become Man. In affirming their doubleness and separate existence, Jesus also establishes, implicitly for now but already with clarity, a hierarchy between the two worlds, of which, however, he defines neither the forms nor the dynamics, even though it is evident that it cannot end with the annihilation of one with respect to the other. The point remains uncertain: it is a crucial "non-finishedness" in Jesus's doctrine, an immense territory to explore—and that is exactly what history would undertake to do.

THE FORCE OF JESUS'S ANNOUNCEMENT lies also in the concrete context of its utterance. His teaching was concluding in front of Pilate (the intuition that the latter "figures in it for essential reasons" is absolutely right): the final moment of his preaching is for the prefect's hearing, and he needed to be before the arrayed power of Caesar so as to declare its relativity and finiteness. The presence of Caesar's delegate is a constituent part of the communication of the message. It is as if Jesus needs Pilate here in order to complete his thought—and everything suggests he was aware of it. Only before the Roman prefect, in the full exercising of his function and of his representation, can Jesus—defenseless and in chains—truly proclaim the separation between the two kingdoms, a distance which for him will soon have the most tragic of consequences, and at the same time affirm, as he has already done and is about to do again, the absolute primacy of the world he comes from over the one that is preparing to slaughter him.

The scene is of unparalleled symbolic power; concentrated in the bare economy of the expressive means—in John's account— is an evocative force that does not let up. The boundless mass of reflections and events that the brief sequence of images and thoughts has generated for two millennia retroacts on its original light, and makes it almost unbearably bright. And it is a scene, as we are realizing even more clearly by describing it, that is entirely convincing historically. Nothing appears out of place. That it occurred—actually and not just in imagination, and even in the terms in which we are recounting it—might be the least important thing of all.

Jesus does not rebel against Pilate, and does not contest his role. He evokes this possibility ("If . . . my followers would be fighting") only to rule it out, straightaway and definitively. He is not a zealot in revolt, nor is he the prophet of an apocalypse that is coming to sweep everything away. He does not have an immediate political goal to achieve: he never has had. And he knows—having said it—that the moment of the end of time is a mystery to all except the Father. The Son himself does not know: an example of the dialectic established within the One. He only knows that it will come ("But about that day and hour no one knows, neither the angels of heaven, nor the Son, but only the Father," writes Matthew). For now, his announcement must reckon with the world there is. The more his lesson looks afar, beyond the horizons of history, the more it is full of realism.

For him the Romans are not the oppressors of his people. Nothing induces us to believe it: the question is foreign to him, and this is one reason why the catastrophic outcome of the revolt of 66 did not sweep away the nascent Christian tradition. Pilate must have perceived it immediately, and have felt reassured, as we shall see: he was not in the presence of a rebel or a fomenter.

For Jesus the Romans are instead the masters of the world, who can print the image of their emperor on the coins of the Jews and take their soldiers from one end of the world to the other, up to the threshold of the Temple. They are the quintessential embodiment of terrestrial power, those who have rendered universal the kingdom which has just been referred to, recognizing its existence and autonomy.

Two points are central in his teaching. One is that the moment of his return to the world—the Second Coming, or Parousia—is not predictable, nor can it be known when the final battle with evil will occur; in the meantime, for humans, the time of waiting begins. The other is that in this duration earthly power has a shape and consistency which is not immediately relatable to God. Jesus's presence in chains before Pilate is the proof of this density, of this irreducible protrusion of the human.

With his behavior, Jesus accepts such a doubling of planes; somehow he legitimates it. He does not refuse Pilate's power; he simply shows its boundaries, erecting before him the other kingdom. The next step is short: if worldly power, in the highest form it has ever assumed—that of the Roman Empire—is not contested, this is because it is acknowledged as having a role, a function, a task. But what? Jesus—at least the Jesus of the Gospels—does not say. Yet with his words and his behavior he creates a space of meaning in which that discourse can and must be completed, for Christianity to become rooted in history. If we wish to remain within the channel of the teaching and of the example of the Master, an answer must be given.

Already in the Second Letter to the Thessalonians, Paul (or whoever, if we must doubt the authenticity of the writing) shows that he was perfectly aware of this urgency. In a very obscure passage, directly linked to the text in Matthew regarding the Second Coming, he seems to assign to the constituted power of humans—in continuity with Jesus's thought—the task of "restraining," through its order, the victory on earth of what he describes as the "mystery of lawlessness." Only when "the one who now restrains"—*ho katéchon*—is removed, can the apocalyptic coming of the "lawless one"—*ho ánomos*—take place, and this in turn will open up the way for the victorious Second Coming of Christ, which will definitively defeat evil.

By opposition, *ho katéchon*, it seems, must be identified with a provisional system of order and of rules, supported by a power capable of imposing it, which the arrival of the Antichrist will turn into its contrary—total lawlessness—before Jesus, upon his return, annihilates him with the "breath of his mouth." Was the Hellenized Paul (or one of his pupils) thinking of the empire of Rome, sustained by an unequalled capacity to unify human beings by dictating to them a universal *nómos* (which was the way the Greeks, from Polybius onward, depicted Rome)? It is hard to say with certainty, but it seems probable to me that he was. If so, we might have a trace of the kind of image Jesus had of Pilate, in front of him in the Praetorium of Jerusalem: the representative of an imperfect and transient order, and yet necessary to the design of the Father, before the coming of chaos and before the final victory over absolute evil. And so began, at that meeting, the long, ambiguous, and complex contest which, for two thousand years, the Church of Christ would never stop playing with the power of Caesar.

4.

"So you are a king?" Pilate asks again. He must have been not a little surprised by Jesus's words. The prisoner did not seem greatly concerned about defending himself from the serious accusations leveled by the Jews, but appeared to be pursuing his own agenda in which it was more important to take the opportunity to reaffirm, loud and clear, some points of his teaching, than to try to make his position less desperate. What is more, Jesus had himself used without hesitation a dangerous word: "kingdom." Admittedly, he did so with a different and disorienting meaning, but it was still a minefield given his alleged crime. The prefect decided to return to the subject again. He could not do otherwise; but he is almost halting in his insistence. He does not draw the conclusions himself, but invites Jesus to make them for him. He does not allude (at least not as reported by John) to what he has just heard about the distinction between the kingdoms. But this confused him. In that "so"—*oukoûn*—which introduces the question there lies an evident hesitation. Everything becomes suspended. It truly is no longer an interrogation prior to punishment; it is a dialogue in which Pilate appears to be increasingly involved and troubled.

"You say that I am a king. For this was I born, and for this I came into the world, to testify to the truth. Everyone who belongs to the truth listens to my voice," replies Jesus (the first part of the answer, "You say," is also in the Synoptics). The issue of regality is quickly closed. The question is overturned: that I am a king is what you said, and so be it. For Jesus there was nothing more to add on that question: what needed to be clarified had already been brought into the light.

Then there is another jump. Jesus seems to change subject, and here too we cannot be sure whether the caesura is due to a break in the Johannine account or whether, in the sequence of the exchange, the prisoner—increasingly less concerned, with the open complicity of his judge, to remain within the limits of what he has been asked, as we would expect in an inquisition—really did move on abruptly to talk about something else.

The theme that bursts into the dialogue in this way is the truth—*he alétheia*. The question of regality was imposed by Pilate. Now it is clearly Jesus who takes over the reins of the colloquy. He is following a clearly defined thread. First he has explained in what sense he is really king, and has distinguished the two fields, of God and of Caesar. Now he is giving substance and content to his kingdom, definitively establishing its primacy. He has come from his world into the human one, himself becoming man ("for this was I born, and for this I came into the world"), only in order to bring the truth to it ("to testify to the truth"). The link with what he has said earlier is inescapable. His is the kingdom of truth—which cannot be said of the kingdom of Caesar—and so anyone on the side of the truth cannot but follow him ("hear my voice").

The truth is identified in this way with the kernel of Jesus's preaching and of his presence among humankind. The primacy of his reign is not therefore a question of power. The kingdom of God is not superior because it displays greater power, but because it is the kingdom of truth. The theologization of morals reaches its peak here. Power is if anything a consequence of truth, but this connection will appear evident only at the end of time, in the final battle with evil. For now, Jesus, in the human world, is the "witness" of the truth (the verb used is *martyréo*), not the one who imposes it. At present the truth divides: not everyone follows it.

Jesus's insistence on this word and the use he makes of it, as if indicating a revealed, absolute knowledge, to be accepted or rejected in its entirety rather than to be critically appraised with doubt and intellect (as prescribed by the cautious Hellenizing eclecticism of the imperial ruling groups, which veered between relativistic skepticism and more confident Stoic rationalism), again disorients Pilate. He has realized he is not in the presence of a hothead blinded by the "superstition" later spoken of by Tacitus, but a figure who stands out sharply from the restless, feverish, and, for him, hard-to-understand backdrop of Jewish religiosity. Before the prefect, Jesus does not say much: in Mark and Matthew reference is made to his long silences during that dramatic morning, and John too (but later) speaks of his muteness. It is quite possible that Pilate now pressed him with other questions, not reported in the fourth Gospel, and that at a certain point, in response to Jesus's obstinate refusal to talk, he exclaimed impatiently, "Do you not hear how many accusations they make against you?"

In such interrogations, a refusal to talk might well have led to torture by the tormentor (*quaestionarius*): "He was interrogated in proportion to his crimes. He was subjected to torture," reads the record of a trial before a provincial governor in a late antique source, when such practices had, if anything, been toned down compared to Pilate's age. Nothing of this kind is reported in relation to Jesus. From the outset, the governor has chosen a different approach—to investigate rather than to grill. The pressure is psychological, not physical.

And so, as if to break the dizzy vortex of the absolute that seems to be gripping the prisoner, he asks, perhaps interrupting him, "What is truth?"—*tí estin alétheia?* It is the high point of the exchange. We are no longer in an interrogation. Progressively, almost without realizing it, we have been transported from a Praetorium of Judaea into a dialogue of Plato.

Still, there is nothing inauthentic or fabricated in this picture. The question arises naturally and spontaneously from what Jesus has said. Moreover, Pilate's behavior has from the start been softer than custom would suggest for cases of this kind, and so his comment does not jar or appear out of place. We cannot say what tone Pilate used, but I believe Nietzsche is off the mark when, in a famous passage, he sees in it "the noble scorn of a Roman before whom an impudent misuse of the word 'truth' was carried on." Pilate is trying to understand, not to crush. He had no need. There is no disdain nor, even less so, is there the "annihilation" (as Nietzsche writes) of Jesus's position and his words, indeed of the whole of the Gospels. Pilate could easily have reduced the prisoner to silence: a criminal in chains, ready to be tortured, who presumes to talk about the truth! Instead, he steers well clear. He takes the prisoner seriously, and merely displays the perplexity of someone who has not understood. Jesus testifies (as he himself has said) that he is in possession of an absolute certainty whose origin and foundation Pilate does not comprehend. The prefect counters therefore with problematic good sense nourished with rationality, the empiricism of someone who knows that there are more things in the world—a world the Romans were fully familiar with, having conquered it—than can be encapsulated by any philosophy (or any religion). His question is not destructive, as Nietzsche makes out; it is genealogical. He places the curiosity of knowledge and the value of doubt against the assertive proclamation of faith. But at the same time he accepts the terrain proposed by his interlocutor. Indeed, with his question, Pilate definitively yields the role of the protagonist in the dialogue to Jesus. He limits himself, as it were, to playing a defensive game. The roles have been inverted.

We do not know if and how Jesus replied: in John's account the dialogue breaks off here. In his own fashion, Jesus has already answered, but Pilate could not have known this. Shortly before the arrest, when a disoriented Thomas asked him what way to follow, given that the disciples would soon be on their own—more or less the same question as Pilate's: how to find the truth—he had said, "I am the way, and the truth, and the life [*egó eimi he odòs kaì he alétheia kaì he zoé*]. No one comes to the Father except through me. If you know me, you will know my Father also."

So Jesus himself was the truth. His presence as Son was revelation of the truth for humans: not his doctrine as a separate organ of consciousness and knowledge, but he himself in his totality, his essence, his example, his choices, the way he acted in the world— in this world. His person represented the point of interference where God met history, becoming human himself. For him the way (toward salvation), the truth (of God), and life (eternal) were all one, because that is how they appear in God's mind: as the unitary reflection of Himself. But observed from the point of view of human beings—and of Jesus as man—that unity was articulated by radiating into history, and was only perceptible through a number of indications. The three words—in which many exegetes have glimpsed (I believe wrongly) an anticipation of the Trinity—were thus at the same time distinct and grafted into one another: salvation as a path toward the truth, the conquest of which leads into the eternal. The theological framework underlying the trinomial—the quality of the relationship between the Father and the Son—was transformed into a crucial practical lesson, in a simple and power-ful reference to loyalty in the hour of separation (if you want to save yourselves, I must never leave your hearts) .

The truth—and nothing else—was the common substance of the Father and the Son. It was this that Jesus preached, or rather, the reflection of it in human history. "I give you a new command-ment," he had said just before, again in John's account, "that you love one another. Just as I have loved you, you also should love one another." And then repeating, soon afterward: "This is my com-mandment, that you love one another as I have loved you." And once again, in conclusion: "I am giving you these commands so that you may love one another." This insistent urging, hammered home to an unprecedented degree, reveals the very strong and powerful perception Jesus had of himself: witness of the truth, insofar as the truth is love. The God who, through Jesus, enters into the history of humankind to show them the way, is a God of love. Love is the only way possible for Him to become history. If humans were able to follow his precept entirely there would be no need for the *katéchon*—for a power that regulates and restrains while waiting for the return of Christ—nor would there be the risk of victory by the disorder of chaos ("the mystery of lawless-ness"), as announced by apocalyptic predictions. It is the lack of love that opens up in history the breach for the laceration of evil.

But that evening—the evening before he met Pilate—Jesus added something further: "No one has greater love than this, to lay down one's life for one's friends." In this way, imminent death took up a place wholly within his preaching, an intrinsic element of his bearing witness to the truth: death as the extreme truth of love. Soon after, as we have seen, he would prevent Peter from using his sword to defend him ("Am I not to drink the cup that the Father has given me?"). If, for Jesus, death became the transfiguration of love, it became, by virtue of this very metamorphosis, a necessary death.

MARK AND MATTHEW SPECIFICALLY STATE that Pilate was "amazed" at the prisoner's conduct (the verb in both is *thaumázein*—an amazement whose semantic field also includes admiration). This detail is missing in John, but the whole of his story is, in a certain sense, a confirmation of the growing surprise of the prefect, who would not otherwise have behaved, in such circumstances, as he decided to do.

It was precisely from Pilate's astonishment that the first turning point of those hours came. Evidently, nothing until then had gone as he had imagined it would, on the basis of what Annas and Caiaphas had told him. He was expecting a hothead, an agitator, a dangerous subversive, a rebel. It is possible that his informers—who had probably had opportunities to listen to Jesus previously, or at least to gather firsthand knowledge about him—had painted a slightly different and less prejudiced picture. But what had happened was totally unanticipated. In the face-to-face meeting, the prisoner's personality must have seemed perturbingly and unexpectedly powerful. Just talking to him had been enough to render apparent the flimsiness of the whole framework of accusations prepared by the priests, which had probably never entirely convinced Pilate. The suspicion—perhaps lurking in him all along—that he was being drawn into a settling of scores between Jewish factions, from which the Roman power did right to steer clear, was now almost a certainty. He would have to extricate himself from the situation with the least possible damage.

Only the Gospel of Matthew relates that the prefect's line of action was influenced by a message sent to him by his wife in the course of the questioning: "Have nothing to do with that innocent man [Jesus], for today I have suffered a great deal because of a dream about him." We know nothing about Pilate's wife, not even whether he had one (in the apocryphal "Cycle" that bears his name, where this episode also appears, she is called Procla). It was not customary for the wives of Roman high functionaries to follow their husbands on provincial postings. Nor can we hypothesize where Matthew found the detail, together with others concerning the condemnation of Jesus which are totally absent in Mark.

Irrespective of these doubts, it is difficult to view such a detail as reliable. Rather, it seems to draw on the literary–religious— also biblical—tradition of the dream as revelatory of divine will, in order to stress the innocence of Jesus: a theme dear to Matthew. It is also possible that the author was reworking, in a Christian key, the narrative model of the Roman matron close to Judaism, which we find, for example, in Josephus (and which is repeated in the apocryphal Gospel of Nicodemus).

It is equally hard to lend credence to another episode, reported this time only by Luke (and here too we do not know exactly where he got it from), in which Pilate, after having questioned the prisoner, decides to send him to Herod Antipas—the son of Herod who had been appointed by the Romans, with the title of tetrarch, as their vassal in charge of Galilee. This was the region where Jesus had been born, and this fact figures as the explanation for the referral. Antipas was himself in Jerusalem at that time for the Passover, and as he had expressed a desire to see Jesus, having heard talk of him, Pilate decided, so the story goes, to satisfy his wish. Antipas interrogated the prisoner at length, but he remained silent all the time. Then, having crudely mocked him, the tetrarch sent him back to the prefect without concluding anything, but in this way consolidating their relationship ("Herod and Pilate became friends with each other; before this they had been enemies").

Nothing in this account holds up. First of all, the temporal frame: on a morning already packed with events, according to the Synoptics and to John, there would not have been time to transfer Jesus to Antipas's residence, even if it was nearby, to which we must add a protracted interrogation and further derision and insults. And then there is the incongruity of the whole affair. Pilate had no reason to refer the prisoner to Antipas. For what purpose? Jesus had been arrested on the territory of a Roman province, and could not leave Roman–Judaean jurisdiction. For the prefect to decide otherwise would have been to forgo his own power of command (we might even say, his own jurisdiction), which would have been totally inadmissible for a Roman governor. Besides, Antipas was a guest on imperial territory; on the basis of what authority could he have taken a decision about Jesus? No Roman rule specified that jurisdiction might be based on the accused's place of birth.

Nor is anything said about a decision by Antipas. Did he find Jesus not guilty as well? Or must we think that Jesus was sent to the tetrarch not to be judged, but merely so that Antipas could meet him, it being taken for granted that he would be returned to Pilate? Interrupting the process of ascertaining the prisoner's guilt, with the Jewish notables waiting outside, for a courtesy visit with no consequences in terms of the inquiry would have been a highly singular course of action.

I believe we need to look in a different direction, so as to uncover the reasons for this unlikely description: to the desire of Luke (or of his source) to amplify as far as possible the Jewish responsibility for the condemnation of Jesus, by involving in the final outcome not only the Judaean authorities but also those of Galilee, the land where Christ had been born—in short, of the whole of Israel. We might also consider the author's probable wish to establish a parallel between Antipas's (invented) "trial" of Jesus and Agrippa I's (historically true) trial of the apostle Paul, showing how the two most important Herodians—Antipas and Agrippa—had been symmetrically involved at the origin of anti-Christian repression.

PILATE LEAVES JESUS, THEN, and once again steps outside the Praetorium, toward the waiting priests. The sun must by now have been high in the sky. Difficult hours lay ahead.

4

THE DESTINY OF
THE PRISONER

✠

1.

The dialogue with Jesus was accompanied, now, for Pilate, by discussion with the Jewish notables gathered in front of the palace. An unexpected situation had arisen, brought about by the conduct of the prisoner, the answers he had given, and the force—evidently perturbing—of his personality. Pilate was no longer ready to accept the guilt of the man under investigation—as perhaps he had been preparing to do—and had decided to inform his accusers of this. Before going outside, did he tell Jesus about the view forming in his mind? Was the latter aware of the governor's inclination? We cannot say, but it is hard to believe—even supposing silence or reticence on the prefect's part—that he did not intuit anything, did not realize that the interrogation was taking a different and, for his accusers, unfavorable turn. How would Jesus have reacted to the direction in which things were going? Heartened, perhaps, like someone who sees the dense clouds over his head suddenly thinning out? It is a crucial question—as we shall see—but for the time being we will leave it in abeyance.

Pilate now addresses the Jews: "I find no reason to condemn him," he says, in John, while Luke is even more detailed: "You brought me this man as one who was perverting the people; and here I have examined him in your presence and have not found . . . any of the reasons for which you accuse him." (We should not be deceived by that "in your presence"— *enópion ymôn*: it does not necessarily mean that Pilate carried out his interrogation in front of the accusers—contradicting John's version—but simply that the inquiry had been conducted while the Jews were waiting outside. Luke's reference to the prefect "[calling] together the chief priests, the elders, and the people," would make no sense if they were all already there.)

Pilate's statement was interlocutory, and not a verdict. It communicated an orientation rather than a decision. Jesus was still in the Praetorium, and the questioning could be resumed at any moment, as in fact it soon would. Could the prefect have gone further and released the prisoner? Of course: he was quite within his powers. But he decided not to, so as not to force the situation. His relations with Annas and Caiaphas were delicate and complex; Judaea was a difficult country; and he knew perfectly well that he was on a razor edge. But even so, his declaration came as a complete surprise to the members of the Sanhedrin, especially to the two high priests, after the negotiations preceding the arrest, which had been expedited with Roman collaboration, and after the hurried nighttime meeting in Annas's house.

A stalemate was forming, charged with a tension we can readily imagine. The governor's words, though cautious, were strong, and there was the risk of arriving at a point of no return. On the other hand, the priests could not back down and drop their accusations without suffering a serious dent in their role and prestige, with unpredictable consequences. We know nothing about what Pilate might have ventured to promise them or the terms in which he did so, nor the instruments of pressure Annas and Caiaphas could bring to bear on him (they may also have alluded to past and perhaps nontransparent forms of complicity), but the priests certainly did not expect such a twist in events. A very real danger existed that a serious crisis might develop between the Roman authorities and the Jewish aristocracy: the nightmare of every good governor (this is what almost certainly led Pilate to be prudent), but also the great fear of every local group of established notables.

Then Pilate had an idea that was entirely political: to search for a solution that would enable Jesus to be saved, while allowing his accusers to back off without overly compromising their credibility. The ploy was to offer an exchange: the life of Jesus for that of another prisoner, whose name was Barabbas—a figure mentioned only in the Gospels.

The Synoptics report the episode, as well as John (who is the most succinct). Historians of law—both Jewish and Roman—have tried at length to identify the legal foundations of Pilate's offer. The most reliable hypothesis, it seems to me, is that there was a custom—possibly of Hasmonean and Herodian inspiration—of pardoning a condemned man during the Passover festivities, and that this tradition had already been acknowledged and respected by Pilate on other occasions. The prefect now tried to turn it to his advantage, on the basis of a subtle calculation, namely, that his Jewish interlocutors would never ask the Romans to free, in Jesus's place, a condemned man whose release would surely be unacceptable to them.

We cannot imagine Pilate's suggestion to have been casual. There were undoubtedly other prisoners waiting to be judged; Jesus would be crucified together with two robbers. Nor can we suppose that a preliminary pronouncement had already been made in Barabbas's favor, and that proposing him was an obligatory course of action. Nothing suggests it; the choice between the two prisoners was entirely an improvisation of the prefect's, a precise and credible trace of which can be found in Matthew: "So after they had gathered, Pilate said to them, 'Whom do you want me to release for you, Jesus Barabbas or Jesus who is called the Messiah?'" (In the most important manuscripts the name "Jesus" is not used for Barabbas, which is a patronymic; this detail should not to be rejected, and it was probably omitted from the principal texts by Christian copyists out of respect for the Son of God.) Otherwise, following custom, the governor would himself have chosen whom to pardon, subsequently making his decision known: a fleeting comment, again in Matthew, that "the crowd" decided whom to free seems unfounded, and is part and parcel of a deliberate falsification wrought by the tradition drawn on by the writer, as we will see very shortly.

So why exactly did Pilate choose Barabbas, who, according to the Gospel, was not a common bandit—among the many at large in Judaea, Samaria, and Galilee? He was something more than that: a "notorious"—*episemon*—prisoner (Matthew), who had committed murder during an insurrection in the city (Mark and Luke); a simple "thief"—*lestés*—only for John. He was, in other words, involved in the anti-Roman resistance: an insurgent, perhaps a Zealot, and certainly a bitter enemy of the Sadducee aristocratic groups, who were accused by rebels like him of abhorrent and sacrilegious connivance with the foreigner. Thirty years later, the same environment that for decades had spawned figures similar to Barabbas—a permanent smoldering insurrection—produced the men who, in the revolt of 66, exterminated the pro-Roman Judaean nobility. Pilate thus believed he had chosen the right person to set against Jesus in order to save him: a subversive whom the priests of the Sanhedrin (he thought) would never spare.

BUT TO WHOM DID PILATE make his proposal exactly?

According to a received notion ingrained in the Western imagination, the choice between Jesus and Barabbas was offered by the governor to the people of Jerusalem—present for the occasion—who unhesitatingly plumped for Barabbas over Jesus. One of the greatest jurists of the last century, Hans Kelsen, basing his view (as he says) on the story we read in John, saw this episode, to which he returned several times, as a painful but clear example of the intrinsically relativistic and nonevaluative nature of every democracy. The "skeptic" Pilate, faced with the fideistic dogmatism of Jesus, acted coherently as a democrat: he "appealed to the people" and organized a "plebiscite" to choose which of the two accused to save, scrupulously abiding by the result. This interpretation set a trend, sparking an ongoing discussion which brushed up against (but without really addressing) a crucial theme: the intrinsic relation between quantity and truth, between number (of voters) and reason, as an almost metaphysical presupposition of all democratic legitimacy.

Yet in John—however incredible it might seem—there is no trace of this so confidently evoked "people." There are "the Jews"—*hoi loudaîoi*, named five times in a brief segment of text—who are identified specifically and unambiguously as the group that had escorted Jesus to Pilate, the members of the Sanhedrin, perhaps accompanied by their servants and by a detachment of the Temple guard. No one else. This identification recurs with total precision in two other points of John's account: once when "the chief priests and the guards" (and they alone) are mentioned as those who shouted "Crucify him! Crucify him!" in reference to Jesus (we will return to this), and a second time, when the "chief priests" (and only them) are recalled as the authors of a declaration of total loyalty to Caesar (we will come back to this as well). So it was to them alone that Pilate offered his alternative.

The "people," for John, were never involved in the affair. It is an absence we must take seriously, given that the fourth Gospel is our best source for reconstructing the events leading to Jesus's death. According to John, everything was played out within a narrow circle: Pilate, Jesus, and the Sanhedrinites—a closed and exclusive triangle.

In the Synoptics, the scene appears to widen to include other protagonists. Let's see how. In Luke, at the beginning of the account, mention is made of a "multitude"—*pléthos*—that took Jesus to Pilate: but the intent here was surely just to indicate the members of the Sanhedrin and the guards. It is then related that Pilate, when he declared Jesus's innocence the first time, before sending him to Herod Antipas, spoke to "the chief priests and the crowds" (*toùs archiereîs kaì toùs óchlous*): an indistinct, passive presence, which probably indicated just the people accompanying the priests—the previously named *pléthos*—who formed a simple backdrop for the actions of the council leaders.

Finally, Luke says that Pilate, after the prisoner's return from Antipas's residence, called together "the chief priests, the elders, and the people" (*toùs archiereîs kaì toùs árchontes kaì tòn laòn*), to further insist on Jesus's innocence. Here there seems clearly to be a new subject. But the reference is encapsulated within a ritual formula: a clause that must have preceded all of the governor's public announcements, without really implying an active popular presence; later on in the account, in fact, it is always and exclusively the priests and elders to whom Luke refers.

In Mark and Matthew—especially the latter—we have a different narrative core. For them, the people, the crowd (*laós, óchlos*), plays a less marginal role. They are, however, still masses manipulated by the priests ("Now the chief priests and the elders persuaded the crowds," in Matthew, and "the chief priests stirred up the crowd," in Mark). How this could have happened, bearing in mind the fraught relations, in those years, between priests and people, between the Sadducee aristocracy and the humbler social orders, both urban and rural, is hard to say, and prompts another

question: accepting that it really existed, who comprised this eva-
nescent crowd which was maneuvered so easily by the leaders of
the Sanhedrin? The most plausible answer is that we are talking
about relatively small groups, perhaps even hired, mobilized in
advance by the priests to back them up in front of the Roman prefect in case of need—at any rate, an insignificant presence which
in no way altered the nature of events.

The best solution seems to be to carry on trusting John's version. All the Gospels stress Jesus's popularity in those days in Jerusalem, into which he had apparently made a triumphal entry. If
there really had been crowds hostile to him in front of Pilate's
residence, this sudden change of mood would be inexplicable, and
in fact it has never been accounted for in a persuasive way.

Nothing remains then but to acknowledge that in those hours
no significant part of the people of Jerusalem gathered outside the
Praetorium; moreover, we have no archaeological evidence for
supposing the existence there of a space that could hold them. The
governor held his tribunal and administered justice publicly outside
Herod's palace; there was evidently an open space—perhaps a court-
yard—able to contain a certain number of people, but not a square
for an assembly. It was a place for relatively small and easily controllable gatherings—no more than a few hundred people, it has been
suggested—and not for holding "plebiscites" (as Kelsen believed).

Lastly, there would not have been either time or motive for
a mass convocation: Jesus had been arrested in secret, in a nighttime *coup de main*, precisely in order to avoid a riot in his support.
Why should we believe that the priests now wanted—or at least
accepted—a sea of people?

We might imagine a crowd formed not for Jesus, but simply to witness the traditional liberation of one of the prisoners, as a quick sentence in Mark would seem to suggest—perhaps friends of Barabbas, who knew of his arrest and hoped for an act of clemency on the occasion. But here too the numbers would have been limited—the Roman garrison would not have tolerated large gatherings in support of an arrested man—with a very particular composition, and therefore not representative of the whole community. Talking of a "democratic" consultation—and of Jesus being brought before the people of Jerusalem—is entirely without sense, either logical or historical.

I believe there are solid grounds for arguing that Mark and Matthew introduced the theme of the "crowd" into their writing—as we have just seen, Matthew refers to it inappropriately also with regard to the custom of freeing a prisoner—for a precise reason, despite the risk of contradicting what they had earlier said about the popularity of their Master. Both were greatly concerned to impress upon their readers that the death of Jesus was the responsibility of the whole Jewish people, and not only of a small group of priests and their acolytes. A passage in Matthew (which we will come to shortly) is revelatory in this respect.

2.

The choice between Barabbas and Jesus was only put, then, to the array of priests, notables, and scribes who, together with the Temple guards, had accompanied the prisoner to the governor's palace. At most, the group may have been swollen by a few clusters of servants, clients, and friends readily controlled by the members of the Sanhedrin, and probably called in by them.

But Pilate had miscalculated, as he must have done not infrequently when it came to testing and appraising the feelings and reactions of what, for him, was such an enigmatic, complex, and unpredictable people, steeped in a powerful culture, with an overwhelming identity, separated by an abyss from the Roman vision of life and the world. Ultimately, he underestimated the degree of hostility felt by the majority of the Sanhedrin toward Jesus.

The priests, when pressed, chose Barabbas.

It cannot have been an easy decision: they were sparing the life of a bitter foe, a man who had not hesitated to take up arms against the aristocrats close to Roman power—a clear indication of just how much the leading members of the Sanhedrin feared Jesus's teaching. Evidently, they regarded the prospect of this inspired and charismatic figure continuing to move freely around Judaea as a deadly threat to their role and position. And there is more. In trying to make sense of events, we must not necessarily suppose that the majority of the council were motivated solely by narrow interests of status and power. Something else, besides, fueled the priests' implacable aversion. They were convinced—rightly—that Jesus's teaching was endangering something deep within the Mosaic religion, of which they legitimately believed themselves to be the custodians, that it was undermining certain essential nodes, to the point of threatening the very existence of their faith: starting with the form of monotheism itself, and its relationship with the tradition of the people of Israel. The crucial link between theological structure and "national" history—the throbbing heart of Jewish identity—was being compromised. The clash was strong, and the stakes extremely high.

So they chose the lesser of two evils: to let go a subversive who, despite his willingness to kill, was, all things considered, of secondary importance and ultimately controllable, in order to eliminate an extraordinary stirrer of consciences, whose continuing liberty might have had incalculable consequences. Let Barabbas live, if it caused Jesus to die. The priests had probably also seen through Pilate's calculation, and wanted the prefect to know it was too late for any change in the game plan. There was nothing to be done now but to press on to the end.

In Luke, who on this point follows Mark and Matthew, an incredulous and disconcerted Pilate repeats his request to the Jews as many as three times ("Pilate, wanting to release Jesus, addressed them again"; "A third time he said to them, 'Why, what evil has he done? I have found in him no reason why he should die'"), obtaining the same response each time: "Crucify, crucify him!" It is an iteration we do not find in John—whose narrative is more terse and rapid, as if already drawn toward the later developments— but which can be considered fairly credible, providing that Mark's and Matthew's versions are shorn of some exaggeration, which makes the repetition seem almost petulant. The governor, in the face of the Jews' obstinacy, would have tried forcefully to prevail on them, in a crescendo of animosity and heated voices. He realized that a dramatic tug-of-war was looming.

At this point, Matthew—and he alone—inserts into his narrative a very famous scene, which casts light on the ideological intent of the tradition drawn on by the Synoptics (but not by John, and by Luke himself with some prudence), definitively clarifying the reasons that had led to the invention of the "crowd." At the Jews' third refusal to free Jesus, Pilate, by now discouraged, "took some water and washed his hands before the crowd, saying, 'I am innocent of this man's blood; see to it yourselves.' Then the people as a whole answered, 'His blood be on us and on our children!'"

Not a single word of this can be believed. Poorly concealed, there surfaces in it, quite distinctly, an overload of prejudice and ideology that takes us straight to what we might define as the zero point in the genealogy of Christian anti-Semitism—to the origins of a Western tragedy.

In the first place, it is unthinkable that a Roman prefect would have chosen to declare his own extraneousness to the unfolding course of events by washing his hands—a ritual that was specifically Jewish and quite foreign to his own culture, both religious and legal, and which, besides, according to biblical tradition, should have come after the killing of the victim, not before. It would never have occurred to Pilate—or to any top Roman official—to behave in such a demeaningly odd manner, even if (and it is by no means certain) he knew about the practice.

And then, that gesture, if it really had been performed, would have had as its obvious consequence the refusal on Pilate's part to carry on dealing with the matter (and in fact, in the fragment of the apocryphal "Gospel of Peter," according to which Jesus was condemned to death by Herod Antipas, Pilate, after having washed his hands, left the place where judgment had been passed). The prisoner would have had to have been immediately handed over to the Jews, who, furthermore, were not permitted to kill him, as we have seen.

None of this happens. Jesus—in Matthew's version as well—stays in Roman hands, and Pilate remains involved to the end, deciding his fate: a serious incongruence which strips the narrative of all plausibility.

In the skillful composition of the text, the episode—constructed for readers not fully aware of Roman cultural diversities—actually served as a premise and a counterpoint for what was said next, which must have constituted the climax of the story: the Jews' dramatic and solemn declaration, "His blood be on us and on our children!" The Jews had to be isolated in their guilt; it was necessary for Pilate to remain out of it. Hence the two symmetrical and contrasting pictures, both in line with biblical tradition: Pilate's washing of his hands (Deut. 21:1–9), and the Jews' complete acceptance of responsibility for what was about to happen to Jesus, according to another ritual formula (Gen. 2:19; Deut. 19:10).

For all this to have the strongest possible sense, the solemn Jewish avowal had to be seen to come not from a small group of conspirators accompanied perhaps by a handful of followers, but from "the people [of Jerusalem] as a whole"—*pâs ho laòs*. The resulting scene is, however, once again completely implausible: a crowd without limit—the whole people—and until then in tumult (so Matthew says: *allà mâllon thórybos ghínetai*), in the face of the unprecedented spectacle of a Roman governor performing with total assuredness a ritual completely foreign to him, responding, in unison, with another biblical formula perfectly symmetrical to the one just uttered by the prefect! A total contrivance, with no fear of the grotesque.

No other purpose, then, was served by the imaginative evocation of the "crowd" and the "people" in the tradition reflected in Mark and, above all, Matthew, than to make the death of Jesus—the deicide—the exclusive responsibility of the Jewish people, of the whole Jewish people (and their descendants), imagined as being present in mass and as a protagonist on the scene of the crime. In this telling, Jesus was not the victim of a conspiracy and did not die due to a Roman decision—Mark and Mathew were probably keen to exclude this responsibility as well—but was killed by an entire people, which had assumed full and collective responsibility for it. In a part of early Christian memory, based on an evident forgery whose genesis cannot be investigated or traced here, a gnawing, corrosive, tenaciously anti-Semitic drive took root, which no exegetic acrobatics could possibly diminish: a deep well of poison that would be transmitted, intact and baleful, down the centuries, preserved in the heart of a memory that became increasingly precious and untouchable.

3.

Pilate went back inside the Praetorium. For John, he had not yet made a decision. According to Luke, on the other hand, he voiced his intentions before retiring: "I will therefore punish him [Jesus] and then release him." This does not seem to me to be a reliable passage. Pilate had just declared he had found the prisoner completely innocent: how could he confirm this conviction and take it through to its extreme consequence ("release him") and at the same time announce he would be punished, albeit not by death? It would be better to think the governor said nothing for now, and that here Luke was just anticipating rather clumsily the succeeding events.

It is likely that the prefect felt uncertain and irritated. His plan had not worked. The Jews' stubbornness had taken him by surprise, and above all he had not foreseen that the priests would dare to oppose him after he had made clear his belief that Jesus was not guilty, arriving at the brink of a risky crisis in their relations with Roman authority.

So he looked for another way out. His goal was still to find a compromise: to save Jesus while at the same time not humiliating the priests and the Sanhedrin, who had been so blatantly forward in demanding the execution of the prisoner. We can suppose he was not a little put out by the obstinacy of the notables. But once again political calculation prevailed over personal distaste.

He therefore decided to inflict on Jesus a castigation that might save his life, at the same time offering the Jews some cause to consider themselves at least partially satisfied: flagellation— a punishment typical of Roman criminal repression during the Principate, especially in the provinces, which could be inflicted either as a preliminary to execution or independently, as a sole punishment. The violence that had already appeared intermittently, albeit not in an excessively heavy way, in the nighttime interrogation, but which had until then remained far from Pilate's

Praetorium, now exploded again, meted out by Roman hands in a more invasive and brutal form.

That Pilate's idea was still to save Jesus emerges in John's account, and also in the mention by Luke we referred to earlier: and it is the most likely reconstruction. In Mark and Matthew, by contrast, the flagellation seems to figure merely as a prelude to the agony on the Cross, but we should perhaps consider this to be a more rushed version, focusing on the facts rather than their connections, which, having recounted what was held to be most important, now moved rapidly toward the end.

Flagellation was a terrible spectacle. Naked and bound, the condemned man would be beaten with varying instruments: a stick for victims of high social rank, whips for slaves or persons of low standing. There was no preestablished duration, nor a specified number of blows, and sometimes the ordeal resulted in death.

We can suppose that Pilate watched the flogging—he was a man of arms, and such things were routine for him—and that Jesus was tied to a column, surrounded by his tormentors, as pictured by the realistic imagination of Caravaggio. We must also believe that—undoubtedly at the prefect's own behest—the suffering did not last long, nor was it particularly harsh, since, immediately afterward, the prisoner was able to stand and, later, to lucidly resume his dialogue with Pilate. In general, such bouts of torture ended very differently.

The punishment was carried out inside the palace. Pilate's plan required that the Jews waiting outside should see the consequences, and realize they were in the presence of a broken man. And so, to the suffering, the blood, and the wounds, the governor decided to add the humiliation of mockery: to take the most dangerous charge that had been leveled at Jesus—his claim to be a king—and to transform it into a pathetic and ridiculous farce. The soldiers on guard put a crown of acanthus on the prisoner's head, which was probably now covered in blood, dressed him in a purple cloak, and hit him again, shouting, "Hail, King of the Jews!" (This detail is in Mark and Matthew as well, though moved forward slightly to just before Jesus is sent off for crucifixion).

There is no doubt that everything took place at Pilate's orders. We are in the Praetorium of Jerusalem, in the presence of the governor: it is impossible to put it down to the excesses of wild, undisciplined troops. This was Pilate's final attempt to get out of a blind alley without too much damage: to display Jesus's devastated condition in order to save his life, and to finally drive home the idea that it was unnecessary to pursue the accusation and continue to demand his head.

So the prefect returned to the waiting Jews: "Look, I am bringing him out to you to let you know that I find no case against him," he declared. Then he showed them Jesus, who had been brought out, probably escorted by his tormentors. He wore the crown and the cloak. "Here is the man," said Pilate—*idoù ho ánthropos*. It is the most dramatic moment in all the Gospels. In its bare essentiality, John's prose achieves great expressiveness. Nothing, if not a wounded and insulted body: and in that body, the majesty and omnipotence of God, disfigured by torturers. The history of Israel itself—both the real and the merely imagined—was condensed in that moment, but transfigured in a universal message of hope and redemption.

Pointing to Jesus, Pilate might once more have proclaimed his innocence, as John recounts. Yet perhaps it is more likely that the prefect tried to present other arguments: the inoffensiveness of the prisoner, at least in political and public order terms—it was precisely for this reason that he had had Jesus flogged and humiliated with the farce of fake regal attire—and then, that he had in any case already been severely and ignominiously punished, and this could suffice. The insistence on proclaiming the innocence of Jesus—which we find in both John and the Synoptics—must belong to a previous layer of writing, perhaps to the Passion story which passed through the hands of all the Gospel authors.

Even this final attempt, however, foundered against the unyielding intransigence of the Jews. The social and physical mortification of Jesus was not enough. "Crucify him! Crucify him," was the only answer given. At this point, in John, a totally incongruous statement is attributed to Pilate: "Take him yourselves and crucify him," he supposedly said to the accusers, "I find no case against him." The reference to crucifixion makes no sense: that was a Roman punishment, which the Roman authority alone—namely, himself—could inflict. The clash with the priests hinged precisely on this issue: that condemnation to death—which they were demanding—could only be imposed by the Romans. Pilate could not possibly have said anything of the kind. The tradition of such an affirmation probably relates once again to the pre-Johannine text mentioned earlier, which was largely inattentive to the institutional and cultural differences between Jews and Romans.

What the prefect must have been envisaging instead—and this explains his interlocutors' next reply, which otherwise would not hang together—was simply handing Jesus back to the Sanhedrin, and letting them do what they wanted: apart from killing him, which was forbidden to the Jews. And it was evidently because they faced such a possibility that the priests were forced to come out into the open and to admit the real nature of the crime committed, in their eyes, by Jesus: "We have a law," they affirmed, "and according to that law he ought to die because he has claimed to be the Son of God" (*nómon échomen, kaì katà tòn nómon ofeílei apothaneîn, hóti yiòn Theoû heautòn epoíesen*).

It is the first time that, before Pilate, the priests say what for them was unsayable: "Son of God." Emerging into the light, finally, is the interweaving of theology and politics that dominated them, the driving force behind the onslaught on Jesus, which the priests had tried to conceal so as to present the prefect with a charge compatible with Roman law, which was totally indifferent to the foundations of Jewish religiosity.

In the agitation of the moment, put under pressure by the governor's unexpected attitude, dismayed by the idea that Jesus might be handed back to them alive in the indifference of Roman power—the worst solution for them—they finally revealed the full extent of their thoughts. Jesus was a sacrilegious blasphemer, who, with his profanity, had placed himself outside the people of Israel, irrevocably moving away from a community that was at once theological and political; for this reason, he had to die. The priests were no longer hiding behind motives of public order in the province, or those of imperial legality. They now invoked what for them was the absolute. And they forcefully asked to be heard by the Romans, who had always declared, ever since Pompey's time, their wish to protect the Jewish cult.

4.

John recounts that, on hearing these words, Pilate was "more afraid than ever" (*mâllon efobéthe*). Both Mark and Matthew (as we saw) reported that, earlier, he was "amazed" by Jesus's behavior. It is evident that Christian memory, through distinct traditions, has preserved traces of the prefect's unusual degree of emotive involvement in the affair. The whole first part of the interrogation, in the version of the fourth Gospel, shows us an inquisitor less and less insensitive and aloof with respect to the prisoner's replies.

But was Pilate really so afraid? And why had the earlier amazement turned into something different and more intense?

I believe John should not be taken literally here, and that we must interpret the verb he uses—*fobéo*—as an abbreviated and easily understandable linguistic sign, in keeping with the essentiality of his writing, to sum up, in a simplified form, what was actually a more complex psychological condition.

For one thing, that scandalous "he has claimed to be the Son of God" shouted out by the priests would certainly have struck the governor. He would instinctively have compared it with the prisoner's behavior—with the exceptional magnetism of his personality, the force of impact of his words. He would have wondered, not without a shadow of apprehension, whether this charismatic figure really was a holy man of the kind often talked about, especially in the East, capable of entering into contact with the invisible—whether he had mysterious magical powers.

Pilate was a Roman of the first century, a man of the imperial establishment: educated enough to reflect upon truth, curious enough to allow himself to be amazed by Jesus, intelligent and clear-headed enough to occupy political posts (and before that, almost certainly, military ones) involving responsibility, discernment, and the ability to make quick decisions. It is probable that he had no solid religious convictions; perhaps something resembling a hazy polytheist eclecticism, possibly tainted with skepticism—it was the climate of the times. This would not have stopped him being superstitious and susceptible to the supernatural, like many Romans, not only in his own epoch. The rationality of the ancients was granular and intermittent compared to the totalizing force of modern reason, and superstition was an enduring mental trait in the history of Rome. Even in more refined social milieus, it was common to find, rubbing shoulders without excessive contrast, credulity and critical realism, dread of the occult and materialistic disenchantment, the implacable logic of legal calculation together with a host of threatening nightmares and remote nocturnal fears. The spread of Pythagorean doctrines, very popular at the time, favored these oscillations, enabling them to be reelaborated in a sophisticated and fashionable way. It was the world of Apollonius of Tyana, but also of the fifteenth book of Ovid's *Metamorphoses,* not to mention many characters present at Trimalchio's dinner, in the *Satyricon* of Petronius, for whom the apparition of specters was perceived to be a genuine problem.

Pilate was not in tune with the Jewish religion: his whole stay in Judaea demonstrates it. He was unable to understand its mindset and power, and must have been mistrustful of the multitude of prophets, preachers, and magic-workers constantly moving around his province—a shadowy sphere of figures on the margins of legality, in his eyes ambiguous and equivocal. Nor can he have appreciated the intransigent doctrinairism of many priestly circles, even those with which he was in closest contact. But he had immediately sensed the diversity of Jesus, the aura of suspended mystery that surrounded him. Above all, the final accusation of the Jews, that Jesus claimed to be the Son of God, heard for the first time in such a direct way—the prisoner had not gone so far during the interrogation, talking only of an invisible "kingdom"—would have made him understand the insuperable gulf now separating Jesus from his accusers, and the impossibility of reaching a compromise.

A sharp sense of disquiet—or, if we like, a confused but persistent perception that something out of the ordinary was taking place before his eyes, a clash with implications he was unable to fully grasp but which he dimly felt to be of massive portent— was combined with an entirely political preoccupation. Pilate had publicly gone to great lengths to sustain the innocence of the prisoner. The Jewish notables had not budged an inch. At the center of the dispute was the inspired and increasingly enigmatic presence of Jesus. What was the way out?

At the end of the day John was right: the word "afraid" may sound excessive to us, but there are several good reasons (we will talk of another one shortly) for believing it was a shaken and troubled

Pilate who went back into the Praetorium, to where the prisoner
had been returned after the fruitless parading of his disfigurement.

THE INTERROGATION RESUMES, but it is like starting from
scratch. Everything has changed compared to the previous
scene. Paradoxically, it is as if suffering violence—flogging,
physical humiliation—had acted in the prisoner's favor, without compromising his dignity or dissipating the efficacy of his
words and silences.

Pilate does not know what to do. He is still entirely convinced
of Jesus's innocence, feels inexplicably involved by his words and
behavior, and is perhaps even tempted to resolve the standoff with
an act of force, though he carefully gauges the risks of such a solution. He addresses the prisoner once again, wanting to understand
more, perhaps hoping that a solution will somehow present itself:
that the idea of saving him might be conclusively reinforced, or,
on the contrary, that some element not yet brought into focus
might emerge to make the accusers' position more acceptable.

"Where are you from?" (*póthen eî sý;*) the prefect asks Jesus.
Even if John had not said anything about Pilate's state of mind, this
question alone would suffice to reveal his bewildered uncertainty,
perhaps even his anguish. From the point of view of the basic facts
and information—geographic provenance, social background,
movements around Palestine—it is evident Pilate had learnt
everything there was to know about Jesus. That is not what he
wants. The origins he would like to discover are different: where

his thoughts come from, the magnetism, the self-mastery, the evocative power of his words, the implacable hatred driving his enemies. The question has an explicitly metaphysical resonance. It is the request of someone who, not without apprehension, senses he is in the presence of the unknown. If Pilate really asked it—and the relationship between the coherence of the account and the conceptual and historical likelihood of the described facts prompts us to consider it possible—the prefect's investigation was no longer centered on ascertaining whether a crime had been committed, but on the nature and mission of the person before him.

Jesus understood full well what Pilate was trying to find out, and remained silent ("gave him no answer"), as he had on other occasions during the questioning. He had already said enough, and felt that no further words were required on this point.

The silence exasperates the prefect, who was evidently already tense. "Do you refuse to speak to me?" he reproaches Jesus. "Do you not know that I have power to release you, and power to crucify you?" (*exousían écho apolŷsai se kaì exousían écho stayrôsai se;*). It is another sign of a slip in control—if not of genuine weakness—on Pilate's part, a clue to the difficulty he faced in keeping a grip on the situation. He had no need to stress the unlimited extent of his power. He was the Roman prefect, in his own palace, surrounded by his soldiers. There were no restrictions on his actions, other than ones he had decided to give himself out of political opportunity or a sense of equity. It was obvious that the life and death of the prisoner depended entirely on the Romans. That he felt the need to reaffirm it demonstrated only his growing sense of insecurity, his concern that events might slip out of hand. His words were directed primarily at himself: an attempt to reestablish the relations of force.

"You would have no power over me unless it had been given you from above"—*ei mè ên dedoménon soi ánothen*—Jesus replies, before adding, "Who, therefore, handed me over to you is guilty of a greater sin."

The realistic eventuality of death—evoked for the first time by Pilate and not just by the accusers—seems to have no effect on the prisoner, as if he took it for granted. It was the foundation of the power paraded by Pilate—the power of Caesar—that interested him. And precisely as it was about to come down on him in the most violent and brutal of ways, he destroys its autonomy and absoluteness at the roots. Caesar and his representative believe that everything is within their domain, but this is only so because it has "been given . . . from above."

Jesus is not returning, from a different point of view, to the theme of the two kingdoms, and the primacy of one over another. He is not dealing with a theological problem of general significance, as he had in the first part of the interrogation. He is now talking about himself and about what will happen to him. It is the specific power of Pilate over him which (in his eyes) is nothing, except insofar as it forms part of God's intention. The prefect's conduct and his position of command are part of a design—this is what Jesus is saying—that goes completely beyond them. The force of the prophesy, the capacity of the Son to see and identify with the will of the Father, erases the uncertainty—not the tragedy—surrounding the choice about to be made. Returning here is the Jesus who, the evening before, at the moment of his arrest, stopped the apostle as he unsheathed a sword to defend him: "Am I not to drink the cup that the Father has given me?" There is no resignation, no negation of the freedom of humankind to decide its own history. Just the will and certainty of knowing: in the eye of God, time is not an unpredictably flowing river but an immobile block of ice, fully perceivable with a single gaze.

The following sentence, the last in the dialogue ("who, therefore, handed me over . . . is guilty of a greater sin"), is thus explained. Jesus, who believes he knows beyond time, completely overturns the relationship with his inquisitor: it is he, in the end, who judges, not the prefect. He is not determining degrees of guilt, but recalling the length of the path that had brought him here; many others had played a greater role in the conspiracy than Pilate, having started it. It is also possible that Jesus never uttered those words, perhaps attributed to him by a tradition which considered it useful to reiterate, whenever the opportunity arose, the Jews' responsibility for what was taking place.

5.

We are now coming to the crucial point in our story, and here, coinciding with this climax, John's account no longer holds up. There is a kind of disjointedness, a blemish in the narrative weft that at first sight cannot be explained. It is worth having the whole passage before us:

From then on Pilate tried to release him [*ezétei apolŷsai*], but the Jews cried out, "If you release this man, you are no friend of the emperor. Everyone who claims to be a king sets himself against the emperor." When Pilate heard these words, he brought Jesus outside and sat on the judge's bench at a place called The Stone Pavement, or in Hebrew Gabbatha. Now it was the day of Preparation for the Passover; and it was around the sixth hour. He said to the Jews, "Here is your King!" They cried out, "Away with him! Away with him! Crucify him!" Pilate asked them, "I shall crucify your King?" The chief priests answered, "We have no king but the emperor." Then he handed him over to them to be crucified.

The first impression is of a change in the rhythm of the narrative, which suddenly, having reached the decisive passage, becomes contracted and rapid, almost anxious to rush toward the conclusion. But let's take a closer look.

There is first of all the sign of a caesura: "from then on"—*ek toútou*, says John (less probably: "thus," "as a consequence of this," with a causal rather than a temporal value—but not much changes), which is followed, immediately afterward, by a statement that does not fit. The turning point purports to lie in the fact that Pilate—from then on—"tried to release" Jesus. What? The prefect had been trying to release the prisoner for some time already, at least since the Barabbas episode. So where was the novelty stressed by John, if in its place we find an expression that seems to allude simply to yet another attempt, with an equally uncertain outcome?

A new development would have existed if Pilate had really decided at this point—without conditions—to free the prisoner, as no one could have stopped him from doing. But if John had wanted to say this, why the precise and inexplicable words, "tried to"? If he simply wished to allude to a further attempt by the prefect, which would have involved more negotiations with the accusers (whom it was necessary to "try to" persuade), there would have been nothing new: Pilate had already done this, without achieving anything. So what was the specifically underlined turning point?

John then adds: "But the Jews cried out, 'If you release this man, you are no friend of the emperor. Everyone who claims to be a king sets himself against the emperor.'" And here the doubts increase, as to both the plausibility of the scene and the position and weight of the accusers' declarations in the train of events.

First of all: where were the shouting Jews? We left Pilate in the Praetorium, with Jesus. The accusers were outside. So did they go in? This is hard to credit. Or did Pilate go outside again, even though John—who until now has recorded all the prefect's movements—says nothing this time? And why should the prefect have gone outside again? To "try" to persuade the Jews to allow Jesus to go free? This would seem the only way to give sense to the account, setting aside the unexplainable reference to the novelty (*ek toútou* might also be thought of as a residual fragment of pre-Johannine writing). This would mean, though, that Pilate had once again opted to try to negotiate—which is difficult to believe. He had already failed twice—once with Barabbas, then with the flagellation—and had nothing more to offer; continuing to insist would have got him nowhere, and he risked seeing his authority being diminished. How can we possibly think he chose this path again? As things stood, Pilate could either accept the request of the priests, or release the prisoner and place before them the fait accompli of his non-appealable decision. Any other possibility appears entirely unrealistic.

There is also the sally of the accusers—"If you release this man . . ."—disregarding for now the question of where they uttered it, inside or outside the Praetorium. The Jews are trying, in a veiled but fairly clear fashion, to intimidate Pilate: if he does not condemn Jesus, he will show himself to be no "friend of the emperor" (a typical expression in the imperial lexicon), and the Jewish authorities might then report him to the legate of Syria, or even to Tiberius in person, for failing to perform his duties and for a lack of zeal in upholding the sovereignty of the *princeps*.

In John's account, the allusion to this threat was seemingly enough to reverse Pilate's orientation, bringing about an immediate shift from the firm intention to free the prisoner (as John himself had just reported) to the opposite and irrevocable decision to condemn him to death. In the narrative economy of the fourth Gospel, there seems to be a direct and exclusive causal link between threat and condemnation, with the outcome of the whole affair resting entirely on the consequences of that single sentence.

But this too is a passage which is very hard to trust. Pilate's position in Judaea, as far as we know, was still solid: if the events took place in 30, as is highly likely, the governor would remain for a further six years in the province—a clear sign that he was firmly established in his post, and felt fairly secure. Above all, the anti-

Jewish campaign being pursued by Sejanus, about which Philo informs us, was in full swing at the time, and a letter or delegation from the Judaeans would probably not have been received well. Pilate must have taken this into account. Matters would be a bit different, certainly, if we were to place the death of Jesus later, after the fall of Sejanus. But not enough.

Admittedly, the idea floated indirectly by the priests might have bothered the prefect, but not to the extent of making him suddenly disavow a view that had been taking shape over hours of questioning the accused and talking with the priests. Pilate also knew full well that to cave in to covert blackmail after such a long and tense confrontation would greatly weaken his standing with the priests; we can see no reason why he should have accepted, given his undoubted position of strength, such a glaring diminution of his role and authority.

It must therefore be conceded that the vague threat contained in the words of the accusers is insufficient, on its own, to support the weight of Pilate's decision, in relation to how events had unfolded up until that moment.

I am unconvinced that things really happened as John tells them. Instead, I think he tried to cover over, with what for him is an unusually disjointed narration, something important and decisive, the true culmination of those hours—there actually was a turning point—which determined, this time for real, the conclusion of the affair, something that Christian memory knew but omitted to say. He concealed it not in the depths but on the surface of his writing, where it might more easily be missed.

To grasp this, let's take a step back in the dialogue between

Pilate and Jesus, returning for the last time to an essential question that has already been raised twice, but left without an answer.

What did Jesus expect from his meeting with Pilate? Did he have a goal and a strategy—perhaps to try to save his own life? And how would he have reacted to Pilate's inclination to release him? What was his state of mind?

Jesus did not want to die, and feared—as we have seen—what awaited him. But he had never thought of any way out with respect to his role and teaching, other than the extreme and total sacrifice of himself. He could not imagine living a peaceful old age in Judaea. He was afraid of the impending ordeal, but certain that he had no alternative. Death alone—that death—could assemble the extraordinary events of his life into a final sequence. Death alone could definitively consign his teaching to history. In the years of preaching, his life—the everyday example—had been indistinguishable from his message. And so dying like this, innocent and tormented, was an integral, nonrenounceable part of it—indeed, the only possible seal. Death was an extremely powerful and definitive sign, which would fix his word forever. His labors would have amounted to nothing if they did not end so. This was the design of the Father, which he was sure—as sure as a man can be—that he had to respect: the death of the Son, who became man for the salvation of all humankind.

So, when he was up before Pilate, Jesus made no attempt to escape condemnation. And every time the situation seemed to take a turn for the better—whenever it looked as if he might be spared—he made no effort to alleviate his position. He knew there would be no let-off, and felt he should not lift a finger to favor any outcome different from his death. He had already behaved similarly at the moment of his arrest, and even earlier, by choosing to go to Jerusalem, where his enemies awaited him. It is an exemplary case of self-fulfilling prophesy: the most sensational in the history of the West, and the most charged with consequences.

I am convinced that from a certain moment onward, the one indicated (and then hidden) by John—*ek toútou*—the governor put all the pieces together into a single picture, fully grasped the prisoner's attitude, and became persuaded—strongly influenced by the man's aura—not to oppose his design. That from a certain moment, a tacit and unspeakable pact formed between Pilate and Jesus, which pushed Pilate in the direction that Jesus regarded as inevitable. This understanding, triggered at a certain point with an irresistible force, determined the final outcome.

It is highly probable that the prefect realized from the start that the arrested man was behaving unusually, a sensation which became increasingly distinct as the questioning proceeded. But it was at a precise instant that the perception turned, for Pilate, into the clear awareness that Jesus, far from wanting to protect himself, seemed instead to be projected toward his own condemnation: the moment when the prisoner, faced with the inquisitor's belief in his innocence and faced, perhaps, with the announcement of his release (suggested in some way by the contradictory words of John), without showing the slightest satisfaction or gratitude for such unexpected support, decided to ignore it. He preferred instead to contest the foundations of the power that was actually declaring in his favor, calling into question the very source of its legitimacy and referring to an inscrutable design of God as the sole driver of what was taking place. Perhaps he went even further, saying (or doing) something else to make it evident that he was certain his destiny did not allow for him to be saved.

And so, I believe, Pilate came to acknowledge—with no possibility for doubt—the end the prisoner wanted to achieve. He understood that Jesus was not stoically superior to whatever might happen to him, that he was not indifferent to his end, but with lucid passion saw death on the Cross as the only possible outcome of his preaching, the final crucial act of his earthly existence, and did not wish to escape it. Pilate must have nebulously perceived such firmness as an unknown and mysterious power ("Where are you from?") unfolding before him, like a numinous sign he was unable to fully interpret but which could not be eluded, and finally decided to accept the unfathomable will of the man before him. So death it would be.

Jesus, for his part, interpreted the encounter with Pilate as the piece still missing in the design of his mission, the extreme point where, once again, teaching and life could be brought together. The presence of the Roman prefect—the representative of Caesar, who had conquered the world—permitted him to reaffirm, with a solemnity and clarity he had never previously reached, some crucial points of his message, and to conclude it in the loftiest possible way. This was his strategy: this is what he expected from the encounter. Pilate was not, for Jesus, the master of his destiny: that was the Father alone. But Pilate provided him with an occasion he rightly judged to be essential: the moment in which to untie, once and for all, the knot holding together in a tangle the whole history of Israel—the conception of God's relation with human power—and to free it into a horizon he felt to be infinitely more vast. To make the Bible not (just) the book of a "national" identity—albeit an exceptional one— but of a universal faith, no longer with any boundaries.

The subjection of Pilate to Jesus's will must in some way have been known to John, as perhaps it must also have been to the early Christian memory reflected in the Synoptics. Those who witnessed the interrogation of Jesus probably saw it straightaway, if Pilate himself did not make it evident, in the final stormy exchange with the prisoner. But it was a hard story to recount, which would have shifted the bare factuality and essential power of the evangelical narratives onto a plane of intentionality and introspection that had deliberately been kept at a distance. It would have brought into play the delicate relationship between predestination and liberty, and would also have obscured what needed to remain quite clear—the responsibility of the Jews for the death of the Son of God.

The suppressed element was not completely erased. Traces remained on the surface of those writings: in John's contradictions, in the irreducible ambiguity surrounding the figure of Pilate and his relationship with Jesus, in the embarrassed suspension of judgment on him, in the unfinishedness that seems to distinguish his profile, through to the birth of the legend—which the Gospels themselves somehow make possible—of a Pilate who was Christian "at heart."

John, who offers the most reliable, rich, and detailed reconstruction of the Passion, comes closest to revealing how things stood. He records the moment of a shift in the interaction between Pilate and Jesus. But then he covers its significance with an incongruous statement. And that is not all: in an attempt to shore up what has just been said, he imagines the Jews intervening with a veiled threat that, on its own, sufficed to induce the prefect to completely reverse his position. He forgets, however, in his anxiety to conceal, that the Jews were outside the Praetorium; nor can he say (as he has always done previously) that Pilate went out to negotiate again, simply because that further phase of discussion never happened, as the search for compromise had already ended with the failure of the flogging.

It is entirely plausible that the priests really did utter the venomous sentence, to allude to the eventuality—in reality fairly remote, but not impossible—of denouncing Pilate. But they must have done so earlier, alongside the declaration that the prisoner had dared to proclaim himself the son of God, before Pilate returned for the last time to the Praetorium to ask Jesus the metaphysical question about his origins. In this way they would have combined, not without a certain rhetorical efficacy, a theological crime (Jewish) and a political crime (Roman), to bring to bear upon the prefect some final, decisive pressure, yet without isolating the threat, transforming it almost into a provocation—as it appears in John's version. And it is likely that in Pilate's troubled state of mind, before he fully realized Jesus's wish and decided to accept it—what John describes as being "afraid"—there was also an awareness of this latter risk: a complaint about him from the Jewish authorities, if not to the emperor in person then to the legate of Syria. This danger could not have been so strong and imminent as to make Pilate change his mind, but it was significant enough to increase his agitation.

6.

Things now speed up. Pilate has decided, and there is no reason to wait any longer. The prefect comes out of the palace (this time he really does, and John does not fail to report it: another clue that the governor had not moved before), bringing Jesus with him, and sits "on the judge's bench"—*kaì ekáthisen epì bématos.*

It is the only moment in which the sequence of events seems to solidify into the rigid formalism of a genuine act of jurisdiction: a decision is about to be made regarding a man's life. Pilate is on the dais (*béma*), where it was evidently customary to administer justice when he was in Jerusalem, in a place—perhaps a court-yard outside the Praetorium—paved with stones (hence the name *Lithostrotos,* meaning "Stone Pavement"), the same in which the Jews had been waiting until then. It is around noon (the sixth hour). The prefect says to the accusers: "Here is your King!" More than sarcasm, as has been suggested, there is a challenge in his words. Pilate wants to show he is unafraid to use the title "king" in front of the priests—and as a fact, in reference to Jesus—after the council members' insinuation that he had not taken sufficient account of the crime contained in the regal claims of the accused. The Jews shout, "Away with him! Away with him! Crucify him!" Pilate answers, "I shall crucify your King." In John's text, there is a question mark after these words. I believe it should be suppressed. Pilate has decided. He is announcing, not asking. Any questions would now be out of place, nor can it be hypothesized that he opened in this way the procedure for a kind of condemnation by popular acclamation, as sometimes seemed to occur in provincial jurisdictions in the East—because of the complete absence of the people in this case. John, right up to the end, keeps reminding us that only the "chief priests" were present. That question mark is probably the addition of an overzealous copyist, if it was not included by the author of the fourth Gospel himself, to soften the crude starkness of that extreme and terrible announcement by hinting at a final, late, and pointless doubt, and once again to ascribe to the priests the "greater sin." They reply, "We have no king but the emperor," forgetting, in the commotion of the moment and in their studied loyalist ardor, that, for them, God alone was the one true king of Israel. They picked up Pilate's challenge and threw it back at him, reiterating their submission to the emperor, as if to say, you are the one who risked damaging yourself due to that name, not us; we handed over Jesus to you in full obedience to Caesar.

John then recounts that at this point Pilate "handed him over to them [the chief priests] to be crucified." Once again the Jews are drawn in unduly: the crucifixion could not have been carried out other than by the Romans, as in fact it was. John himself says so when, later on, he mentions "the soldiers" as the executioners.

But Pilate had the last word on Jesus's regality—a further indication that the title really was at the center of a silent, covert battle between the prefect and the Jews.

After the condemnation, Pilate wrote, or probably dictated, a brief text—in Hebrew, Latin, and Greek, as John scrupulously specifies—for an inscription to attach to the Cross: "Jesus of Nazareth, the King of the Jews." The chief priests tried to contest his choice of words: "Do not write, 'The King of the Jews,' but, 'This man said, I am King of the Jews.'" They had clearly understood the sense of the use Pilate was making of that name: a recognition, albeit paradoxical (with that "your King," repeated twice), that emphasized the victim's irresistible superiority to his accusers, which no condemnation could cancel out.

But Pilate is scornful. He has accepted as a mystery Jesus's will not to elude death, has adjusted accordingly and perhaps fearfully, has been irritated and worried by the obstinacy of the priests, and yet he is still the prefect of Judaea, and no one can prevent him from making that extreme gesture of respect and at once of insolence. "What I have written I have written," he says, perhaps even directly in Latin: *quod scripsi, scripsi.* His day was finished. Not yet that of the prisoner.

ALL THE GOSPELS RECOUNT—with some differences and perhaps, in John's text, interpolations—that after the Crucifixion Joseph of Arimathea, a Jewish notable who was a member of the Sanhedrin and a secret follower of Jesus, went to Pilate "boldly" (says Mark) and asked for the return of the Master's body so he could be buried. The prefect granted the request without hesitation—and this was the way he took his leave of the prisoner. According to Matthew, he also authorized the tomb to be guarded until the third day.

5

INTO THE DARKNESS

✢

1.

Immediately after the events of that morning, the life of Pilate slips back into shadows no less dense than those which had previously enveloped it.

The condemnation and death of Jesus had undoubtedly been a significant moment—and perhaps also something more—of his work in Judaea. We can suppose the image of that compelling, magnetic preacher, and the emotions he had stirred, remained long impressed on his thoughts. The mobilization of all the eminent priests in Jerusalem to ask the Roman authorities to carry out a crucifixion cannot have been a frequent occurrence. He could not possibly have intuited the unparalleled importance of what had happened—the new religion was just beginning its course, gathered around first memories still to be fixed in the Gospel writings—but there is no reason to lend credit to the ferociously anti-Christian imagination of Anatole France when he pictures Pilate in his old age, unable, however much he tries, to recall this distant episode.

In all probability the governor immediately informed Tiberius, sending him a detailed report. A passage in Tertullian, one of the first great Christian authors, in a work composed at the end of the second century, takes for granted the existence of such a document, not to be confused either with the apocryphal writings known as the *Acts of Pilate*, dating to the fourth century (which have come down to us), or with a further hypothetical text by Pilate—of highly dubious existence—to which Justin (another Christian thinker) seems to refer in almost the same years as Tertullian's work.

The testimony should not be downplayed, as some scholars have tried to do. The writer is usually knowledgeable about the customs of the imperial offices; besides, the practice of directly informing the emperor of significant events that had occurred in their territories, and associated decisions, was far from infrequent for provincial governors between the first and second century (Pliny's correspondence contains a well-known example, and precisely in relation to Christians). There was also a certain attention toward Judaea and its religion in Rome during those years: Pilate must have known that, and would have thought it best not to keep quiet about what had happened.

Above all, he had an additional reason for informing Tiberius: to preempt any initiative by the local notables who, as we have just seen, had indirectly alluded to this, albeit only if they did not get what they wanted. The events of that morning—with the tense confrontation between prefect and priests—had, it can be believed, soured their relations, and Pilate would have considered it prudent to cover his back and be the first to act.

What the governor wrote to Tiberius we cannot guess. But the hypothesis that he painted Jesus in a not entirely unfavorable light, though having to justifying his condemnation, should not be dismissed. Pilate did not think like the scathing Tacitus; otherwise, Tertullian would have had no reason to recall the document. The prefect would probably have stressed the unrelenting doggedness of the Jewish religious leaders, and the inevitability of the crucifixion, while omitting what for him was the dominant reason for it. But he would also have been careful not to be too negative about Caiaphas, whom he kept on as chief priest until the end of his mandate; if there was a crisis between them as a result of the wrangle over Jesus, it must soon have been overcome, in the interests of mutual convenience and cautious political realism.

THE DARKNESS WHICH, FOR US, surrounds Pilate's final years in Judaea is briefly broken just twice. And both fleeting glimpses concern his ever-difficult relationship with the Jewish religion.

The first comes to us thanks to a recollection of Philo, already spoken about at the beginning of this book: the oldest testimony regarding Pilate, datable to 41, the year of publication of *On the Embassy to Gaius*. The theological–historical pamphlet arose from a mission made by Philo to Emperor Caligula between 39 and 40, with the aim of persuading the *princeps* to exempt the Jews from certain obligations relating to the imperial cult. One passage includes a letter apparently sent to Caligula by Agrippa I, the grandson of Herod the Great and heir to Herod Antipas in the tetrarchy of Galilee (he would then briefly rule Judaea itself, until 44). In it, besides the harsh judgment of Pilate's prefecture that we have already discussed, a particular episode is described as proof of his misgovernment.

Probably based on a text written by Agrippa (Philo knew him personally, as he was a family friend), the letter can be considered to have been reworked by Philo to reflect his own thinking. We read in it that Pilate installed some gilded shields in Herod's palace in Jerusalem—the same place where he had encountered Jesus. They "did not bear images, or anything else prohibited [by Jewish precepts], except for a very brief inscription indicating two things: the name of the dedicator [Pilate] and that of he who was honored [Tiberius]." But the Jews, when they found out—"it was now on everyone's lips"—took offense, and formed a high-ranking delegation to request that the governor remove them. Pilate, the account goes on, refused, so as not to compromise his tribute to Tiberius, prompting fresh remonstrations from the Jews—"Don't set off a revolt! Don't provoke war! Don't destroy the peace!"—accompanied by the stated intention to send an embassy to Tiberius. The prefect, fearing that a Jewish delegation might also reveal his other misdeeds, wanted to back down, but did not know how. The Jews, meanwhile, wrote to the emperor, begging for his assistance in these difficult circumstances. The *princeps* (concludes the letter), after harshly reprimanding Pilate, decided for the best: to move the shields from Jerusalem to Caesarea, where they would no longer be cause for scandal.

As is immediately apparent, the episode resembles in many ways the incident of the imperial effigies carried into Jerusalem by the Roman troops on their standards, and it has been conjectured that they are one and the same event, recounted in different ways and with varying details by Philo (Agrippa) and Josephus. This hypothesis cannot be entirely ruled out.

The first thing revealed by the text is of biographic significance. When Philo composed the work, but probably also when Agrippa sent his letter (around 38–39), Pilate must already have been dead, or at any rate so isolated and disgraced that he could no longer counter the accusations leveled against him. Otherwise, Philo, and to an even greater extent Agrippa, men close to the imperial entourage and who were extremely sensitive to shifting balances, would have been much more guarded.

As for the time frame of the incident itself—if it is not the same as the one we find in Josephus—I am inclined to agree with those who propose a fairly late dating, after the death of Jesus. The account hints at the possibility of a Jewish embassy to Tiberius, and refers to a favorable reply from the emperor himself to the petition sent by Jewish notables from Jerusalem: events not readily imaginable in the years prior to Sejanus's death, in 31. We have already referred to the anti-Jewish attitudes pervading imperial policy in that period (the information comes from Philo himself). Besides, Agrippa's letter presupposes a lengthy stay by the prefect in Judaea, unjustifiable if the episode had occurred at the beginning, or at least in the first phase, of his mandate (this latter observation also suggests that the incident was not the same as that of the standards). I believe that the most plausible dating is in the years immediately after the fall of Sejanus, let's say after 32.

As we noted earlier, the core of Philo's (Agrippa's) narrative superimposes onto the historical portrait of Pilate—never, in fact, really taken into consideration—the stereotypical image of the bad governor. It does not describe a character, but fixes a type: the high-ranking official hostile to the Jewish religion. In the decision to lambaste the prefect by resorting to a stock judgment, something real does emerge: Pilate's evident difficulty in engaging with the world of the Bible and its tradition. We have seen that his whole period in office in Judaea was marked by this incapacity. Nor can we exclude the possibility that he was struck by Jesus precisely because he was so far removed from the religiosity of the Sadducees and the Pharisees.

What jars, compared to the picture painted by Philo, is the tenuousness of the blame attributable to Pilate, which not even Philo (Agrippa) can accentuate all that much. The governor (after the incident with the standards, we must presume) had been very circumspect: the shields bore no images, or anything else that might disturb Jewish sensibilities, as Philo himself admits. Probably what caused offence was the reference, in the dedication, to the divinity of Augustus, mentioned in relation to Tiberius (named, according to custom, as *divi Augusti filius*, "son of the divine Augustus"). It was not a serious failing, and Pilate himself, perhaps after some dithering, declared his willingness to remedy it. But the notables had already written to Tiberius. The tone of the emperor's reply is clearly exaggerated by Philo, again for nakedly ideological motives: to show the emperor's sympathy—

now free from the baleful influence of Sejanus—for the Jews. If Tiberius had been really troubled by Pilate's behavior, he would not have hesitated to remove him; instead, the governor remained in his post for years to come.

What reemerges here is a motif that we now know well: Judaic hypersensitivity—perhaps exaggerated here for political ends—and Pilate's cultural deafness, something akin to a genuine anthropological denial. The passage of time, and the governor's inevitable familiarization with the customs of his province, did nothing to soften a dense layer of incomprehension that kept resurfacing. This incapacity would distinguish Pilate forever in the eyes of the Jews: more guardedly in Josephus, with greater force in Philo, while to the early Christian tradition that same insensitivity would not have appeared so very serious. This is why the image of the prefect that Philo conveys mirrors the one Pilate probably formed of the Jewish world: the sign of a reciprocal and unsurmounted difficulty in understanding each other.

2.

The final known episode about the life of Pilate takes us back to Josephus, who speaks of it in the eighteenth book of the *Antiquities* (there is no parallel in the *Wars*), after having reported the other events concerning the prefect. We are at the end of the governor's mandate, between 35 and 36. The location is Samaria, a largely mountainous area in the north of the province, between Judaea and Galilee. Josephus's portrayal of its inhabitants is not positive: Jewish apostates, ready to change loyalties as circumstances demanded, he writes, probably reflecting a widespread prejudice.

The facts are these. A man—no name is given—described as a lying demagogue gathered together a multitude of devotees and incited them to climb Mount Gerizim, near the city of Samaria— holy according to popular tradition. He promised to show them precious reliquaries, buried on the site by Moses himself. The men armed themselves (an odd decision, in the context of the story) and, growing ever larger in number, camped in a place called Tirathana, some distance from the mountain, and prepared to climb it. They were, however, thwarted by Pilate, who, having occupied the summit with heavily armed units—both infantry and cavalry— launched an attack, killing some and putting the rest to flight.

Then the repression began: many of those who had taken part in the gathering were reduced to slavery, and the leaders summarily executed. In response, the council of Samaritans (the assembly of the region's notables, acknowledged by the Romans), sent a mission to the legate of Syria, Vitellius, accusing Pilate of having carried out an indiscriminate massacre. They claimed that those who had assembled had not done so in opposition to Rome, but only to escape harassment by the governor.

The religious aspect of the incident is less marked this time, although not entirely lacking. Certainly, the origin of the movement seems once again to have been associated with matters of worship, but the man who inspired it did not have—at least in Josephus's view—any credibility on this plane. There is also, and above all, the decisive detail that the Samaritans were armed. It is hard to see why weapons were needed to go hunting for reliquaries left by Moses.

The assembling of a crowd, however large or small, for some unknown reason armed, and led by an ambiguous and discredited figure, was absolutely intolerable from the Roman governor's point of view, and could only be interpreted as insurrection. Moreover, the Samaritan council itself recognized the political significance of what had happened, when, in the embassy to Vitellius, they no longer referred to the alleged religious reasons for the gathering but admitted its explicitly political motivation: to contest, by force if necessary, the governorship of Pilate.

The prefect's initial military response thus appears to have been appropriate: a situation that posed a danger for the public order of the province was arising, and it had to be nipped in the bud. In the light of this objective, the response was swift and effective, and the action well conducted in military terms, anticipating the moves of the hostile forces, which were quickly routed with the best Roman operational protocols: further proof of Pilate's familiarity with war.

It is possible that the subsequent—and at least in part inevitable—repression ordered by the prefect in Samaria was unnecessarily brutal and ruthless. Perhaps it was precisely the memory of this last episode that prompted Philo to accentuate his stormily dark portrait. According to the notables there was even "a massacre"—the word used by Josephus is *sfaghé*. Their argumentation before Vitellius was subtle and well presented. They did not conceal the explicitly political nature of the event, but skillfully channeled its significance in a less dangerous and nonsubversive direction: the Samaritans had not been contesting the sovereignty of Rome, just trying to evade the unreasonably harsh and overbearing government of the prefect.

We have no means of judging the validity of the accusation: Josephus himself reports it with a certain prudence, without commenting on or adding any personal evaluation. The line of defense adopted by the Samaritans might have contained some seeds of truth—and it must have seemed so to the legate of Syria. Pilate was immediately invited to absent himself—albeit perhaps only temporarily—from his post, after ten years, and to go to Rome to account for his actions before the emperor. His place was taken, briefly, by a Marcellus about whom we know nothing else, presented by Josephus as "a friend" of Vitellius—probably one of his closest aides.

It is by no means certain that the legate of Syria considered Pilate guilty: referrals to the *princeps* did not have this significance. Rather, he would have thought it necessary to give some satisfaction to the Samaritans; balanced good sense, not without a streak of hypocrisy, was intrinsic to imperial policy in the East. It is possible he had received other complaints about the behavior of the governor, whose relations with the world of his province—even with aristocratic and tendentially pro-Roman circles—had not always been peaceful, as the condemnation of Jesus has shown. Maybe there had been other unjustified executions. Luke talks of "Galileans whose blood Pilate had mingled with their sacrifices." But this is so fleeting a remark—and has nothing to support it outside of Luke's Gospel—that we cannot glean anything reliable from it; all we can say is that it must have occurred before the death of Jesus—and hence in a distant and hazy past with respect to the time of the Samaritan delegation—probably on the occasion of a pilgrimage to Jerusalem (the reference to sacrifices suggests this; besides, Galilee was not part of the province of Judaea, so the spilling of blood would have taken place outside the land of origin of the victims, and might have been the cause of the enmity between Pilate and the tetrarch of Galilee alluded to, again by Luke, in the invented episode of the sending of Jesus to Antipas).

It is impossible to say what Vitellius made of the Samaritans' complaint. He had not been in Syria long (perhaps no more than a year), and he might not have been displeased by the prospect of a new governor in Judaea. The impression given by Josephus's account is that he seized the opportunity to bring forward a change in the neighboring prefecture which he perhaps considered overdue. A decade was a very lengthy period to be in an office of that kind: although it was an indication that Pilate was judged to be doing a good job, there was still the risk of an accumulation of tensions and grudges, and of a buildup of unhealthy networks of interest and privilege at odds with the practices of good government. It would have seemed right to the proconsul to draw the emperor's attention to such a remarkably long posting, while at the same time providing him with a good reason for a substitution which he judged, at the very least, to be opportune.

3.

Josephus recounts that Pilate set out immediately for Rome, in compliance with Vitellius's orders. It was winter—that of 36–37—and

the sea was "closed," so the prefect had to embark on a long and tir-
ing overland journey through the Middle East and Europe. Before
he reached the capital—as we are again told by the *Antiquities*—
Tiberius died, on March 17 of 37. From that moment on, nothing
more is known about Pilate. He simply exits from history: suddenly,
just as he had entered it. His visibility coincides for us with his presence in Judaea. The only reliable information, as we have said, is
that around 40 he must already have been dead, or at least reduced
to silence.

The void is filled with legends and apocrypha, which accompanied the spread and definitive affirmation of Christianity in the
West and in the Byzantine world: a markedly positive judgment
by Tertullian (in the text just mentioned) seems to dissolve in later
tradition—from Origen to Eusebius to Ambrose to John Chrysostom, and to Augustine himself—marked by a fuzzier and more
prudent evaluation. Various stories soon began to circulate about
Pilate's end, in particular, in which layers of popular folklore can
still be distinguished from more sophisticated elaborations with
complex allegorical frameworks. In one of these invented tales,
the emperor condemned his former prefect to live in a cave,
which the *princeps* himself happened upon one day while hunting
a gazelle. The animal stopped right in front of the recluse's abode:
Caesar immediately loosed off an arrow at his prey, but it flew
through the entrance of the cave and killed Pilate.

According to another tradition, known also to Eusebius (but
not to Origen, who died around 254, about ten years before Eusebius was born, which is perhaps a clue for dating it), the prefect
committed suicide: "It is worthy of note that Pilate himself, who

was governor in the time of our Savior, is reported to have fallen into such misfortunes under Caligula . . . that he was forced to become his own murderer and executioner; and thus divine vengeance, as it seems, was not long in overtaking him." Even his lifeless body attracted attention and stirred the imagination: one tale has it that he was thrown into the Tiber, but then fished out and taken to Vienne, in the south of France, in Narbonensian Gaul, ending up in the Rhône, and later, in the Lausanne region: and each of these steps was marked by fatal and diabolic events. In yet another version, Pilate was decapitated by order of the emperor, but then forgiven by Jesus, who accepted him into heaven with his wife Procla—also mentioned, but not named, in the Gospel of Matthew.

As for the apocrypha that go under his name, the first figure who seems to have known about the existence of the *Acts of Pilate*—a set of documents attributed to the prefect, not to be confused with the report, which we presume to be authentic, sent by Pilate to Tiberius and recalled by Tertullian—is Justin: but he had not consulted them directly, and his testimony only proves that when he was writing his *Apology*, around the middle of the second century, a forgery already existed, or at least rumors circulated about one. In the fourth century, Eusebius and Rufinus cited a dossier with strongly anti-Christian content, which also went under the name of Pilate—another falsification—about which, however, nothing is known.

The *Acts of Pilate* that have come down to us are usually included by editors, together with another text about the "descent into hell," in the so-called Gospel of Nicodemus, and are essentially an account of the Passion, Resurrection, and Ascension of Jesus, strongly anti-Judaic in tone and probably composed between the fifth and sixth century. They are transmitted by way of two manuscript traditions, indicated as A—more complete—and B, narratively less rich; versions exist in Latin, Coptic (these two mainly follow the Greek text A), Syriac, and Armenian.

Pilate plays a positive role in them: he would like to conduct a rigorous inquiry, tends to privilege testimony favorable to Jesus, and yields only in the face of the increasing exasperation of Jewish pressure. But in this modest, confused, and dark account we are unable to find a single significant piece of information useful for reconstructing the biography of the prefect and his views. All we have is a document illustrating the fervor of the ideological battles waged in the East around late antique Christianity, probably intended to contrast with other apocrypha, about which we know nothing.

Finally, there is a further series of apocrypha—known as the "Pilate Cycle"—written between the seventh century and the Renaissance, which reproduces, among other things, letters exchanged between Pilate, Tiberius, and Herod Antipas, an account of the arrest of Pilate by Tiberius, and the report which the prefect seems to have sent to the emperor about the death of Jesus (in fact, just a clumsy summary of some chapters from the Gospel of Nicodemus). These documents, like the others, are of very little value for the historian of antiquity.

Nonetheless, it is useful to consider these texts. From the labors—often ingenuous and openly biased—of those who constructed them, there emerges, with increasing insistence, a subtle

but perceptible sensation that accompanies from the start everyone seeking to approach the Gospel figure of Pilate. The falsifiers,
in dealing with the few available sources on the prefect of Judaea,
seem to have absorbed the patina of the originals, and transmitted, dilated through reworkings, the same unmistakable tone.
The impression conveyed is of an insuperable obscurity which
forms around Pilate as soon as he is talked about; his key feature,
it seems, could be nothing other than the undefined, a fog—as if
he were enveloped by the shadow of an unsaid, of an unstated,
that intercepts the light each time, or deforms it.

This is true above all for the Gospel of John, not by accident
the one which falsifiers, over the centuries, have borne most in
mind. As if the oldest Christian tradition had been the custodian
of a secret about Pilate that could not be revealed, but could not
be entirely removed either; a secret that has faded over time,
becoming completely lost, but which has left behind it a long trail
of opacity.

The victory of Christianity, its affirmation as the universal
religion of the Roman world, produced incalculable effects on the
fabric of its early memory. In the space of a few decades, Christians
went from being a persecuted sect to being absolute protagonists
in the cultural and political life of what continued to be a great
empire. Their whole past was thus rethought in the light of the
turnaround that occurred at the beginning of the fourth century.

In the trauma of such a sudden and profound reconversion,
the truth about Pilate, the truth of his behavior before Jesus—
perhaps already less clearly remembered—was definitively lost.
But there remained, to evoke it, a wake of mystery that would

never dissolve, a perception of intermittence, almost of suspension, which would shroud for ever, in the eyes of posterity, the figure of the fifth prefect of Judaea.

TERTULLIAN DESCRIBED PILATE, in the text just recalled, as "a Christian at heart"—*pro sua coscientia christianus*. It was a bold appraisal. Why was it proposed? What was he trying to say? On what grounds did Tertullian make his judgment? A reading of the Gospels alone could not authorize him to venture so far. From where did he draw his information?

I believe he had information that we do not—that he was aware of a tradition in which Pilate's behavior was explained for what it had been: a surrendering to the power of Jesus's prophesy about himself, to the inevitability of the prisoner's death. It was a truth hard to relate, that might easily be misunderstood and break that delicate equilibrium between free will and the foreknowledge of God—between Jesus's human and divine nature—which made the sacrifice of the Son an incomparable tragedy, and not the performance of a preestablished script. To avoid this risk, some culprits for that death, who had been free to decide, needed to be found. The choice could not remain other than ambiguously open: it was a toss-up who was to blame, Pilate or the priests, leaving aside the idea, which took shape straightaway, of shifting responsibility onto the whole people of Judaea. If it had been admitted that the prefect yielded to what he understood to be the manifest will of Jesus, the way would have been paved for scores of interpretations, all potentially misleading with respect to the new religion, which might have diminished the value of that unparalleled gesture: the martyrdom of the Son of God for the salvation of all humankind.

That shocking yet so reasonable truth—of a tacit understanding, favored by the asymmetry between the two interlocutors—had to be concealed, masked by tales which tried to deflect attention and prevent it from being perceived, even at the cost of making the entire event almost inexplicable, and of casting upon it—at least on the side of its minor protagonist, Pilate—the shadow of the incomprehensible.

I believe, however, that its deciphering remained in the air for some time, invisible due to its very transparency, but not completely erased. And when the Nicene Creed was reformulated in Constantinople at the end of the fourth century, and it was decided to add to the recollection of the death of Jesus the name of Pontius Pilate—without indicating him as responsible for the crucifixion—I do not think this was done (as is usually said) merely to establish a chronology (if so, it might have been more appropriate to name Tiberius as well). Something more substantive underlay it: the by then distant echo of a memory, of a matter to settle, a truth not to be entirely lost. Those names had to go together, as on that morning when everything unfolded. Forever.

SOURCES AND
HISTORIOGRAPHY

✠

I. The Ancient Tradition

The most important sources on Pontius Pilate are Josephus and
the Gospels, to which we must add Philo, Tacitus, Tertullian, and
an epigraph discovered in Caesarea.

The texts I have cited by Josephus do not present particular
critical problems, with one exception, the so-called *testimonium
Flavianum,* discussed in chapter 2. They belong both to the *Wars
of the Jews,* in seven books—originally composed in Aramaic,
and then rewritten in Greek between 75 and 79, with the help
of assistants possessing a greater mastery of the language than
the author—and to the *Antiquities of the Jews,* in twenty books,
also written in Greek with the aid of assistants, and completed
between 94 and 95. The fundamental edition is still Benedictus
Niese, *Flavi Iosephi Opera,* 6 vols. (Berlin: Weidman, 1888–95,

reprint 1955: *Antiquitates*, vols. I–IV; *Bellum*, V–VI); the one of Samuel Adrian Naber, in the Bibliotheca Teubneriana series, *Flavi Iosephi opera omnia*, 6 vols. (Leipzig: 1889–93: *Antiquitates*, vols. I–IV; *Bellum*, V–VI), should be borne in mind as well. The Loeb edition, edited by Jeffrey Henderson, is also excellent, and was drawn on, with some minor modification, for the translations in this book: *Wars* (Cambridge: Harvard University Press, 1927, reprint 2004), translated by H. St. J. Thackeray, and *Antiquities* (Cambridge: Harvard University Press, 1965), translated by Louis H. Feldman. For insight into the world of Josephus: Santo Mazzarino, *Il pensiero storico classico*, II, 2 (Bari: Laterza, 1966), 95ff.; Pierre Vidal-Naquet, *Flavius Josèphe ou du bon usage de la trahison* (Paris: Les Éditions de Minuit, 1977); Shaye J. D. Cohen, *Josephus in Galilee and Rome* (Leiden: Brill, 1979); Tessa Rajak, *Josephus: The Historian and his Society* (London: Duckworth, 1983); Per Bilde, *Flavius Josephus between Jerusalem and Rome: His Life, his Works and their Importance* (Sheffield UK: Sheffield Academic Press, 1988); J. Carleton Paget, "Some Observations on Josephus and Christianity," *Journal of Theological Studies* 52 (2001): 539ff.

A great deal of study has been devoted in modern New Testament criticism to the structure of the Gospels, the invention of their form, and the stratification of their sources: for a preliminary orientation, Raymond E. Brown, *An Introduction to the New Testament* (New York: Doubleday, 1997), and Gerd Theissen, *Das Neue Testament* (Munich: C. H. Beck, 2002). I accept the now widespread view that the most ancient text is Mark, the shortest. It was composed between 60 and 70 (whether before or after the Great Revolt is subject to debate), in a place that cannot be identified with certainty (Jerusalem, Alexandria, Antioch, Rome even), and must be considered as being the closest to the oral tradition, in which the first shift from Aramaic to Greek had probably already taken place following the conversion of communities that spoke (only) this language. Written documents must however have been circulating for some time, both in Aramaic and in Greek: collections of Jesus's sayings, parables, descriptions of his miracles, and an account of the Passion—the first of the traditions about Jesus to be wrought into a genuine narrative fabric—known to all the evangelists: Martin Dibelius, *Die Formgeschichte des Evangeliums* (Tübingen: Mohr, 1919), especially 15ff. and 56ff., in English as *From Tradition to Gospel* (London: Ivor Nicholson and Watson, 1934), is an extremely important book (not only from the point of view of the "criticism of forms"), which should be read together with Rudolf Bultmann, *Die Geschichte der Synoptischen Tradition* (Göttingen: Vandenhoeck & Ruprecht, 1921), in English as *The History of the Synoptic Tradition*, translated by John Marsh (Oxford: Blackwell, 1963), another study of particular significance. Also worth remembering are Karl Ludwig Schmidt, *Der Rahmen der Geschichte Jesus* (Berlin: Trowitzsch, 1919); Vincent Taylor, *The Formation of the Gospel Tradition: Eight Lectures* (London: Macmillan & Co., 1933, 2nd ed. 1935), especially 44ff., and Id., *The Gospel According to St. Mark* (London: Macmillan & Co., 1963); Willi Marxsen, *Der Evangelist Markus: Studien zur Redaktionsgeschichte des Evangeliums* (Göttingen: Vandenhoeck & Ruprecht, 1956), in English as *Mark the Evangelist: Studies on the Redaction History of the Gospel*, translated by J. Boyce et al. (Nashville: Abingdon, 1969). And, more recently: Rudolf Pesch, *Das Markusevangelium*, 2 vols.

(Freiburg: Herder, 1977–78); Joachim Gnilka, *Das Evangelium nach Markus*, 2 vols. (Zurich-Neukirchen: Benziger, 1978–79); Werner H. Kelber, *The Oral and the Written Gospel: The Hermeneutics of Speaking and Writing in the Synoptic Tradition, Mark, Paul and Q* (Philadelphia: Fortress Press, 1983); Martin Hengel, *Studies in the Gospel of Mark* (London: SCM Press, 1985).

In Matthew and Luke—which, with Mark, form the so-called Synoptics—there is both the nucleus of Mark and, for the amplifications, a common source (unknown to Mark) generally denominated Q ("Quelle"), lost to us, probably precisely because it was completely absorbed into the Gospels. Both also drew on other material, of uncertain provenance: see John S. Kloppenborg, "L'Évangile 'Q' et le Jésus historique," in Daniel Marguerat, Enrico Norelli, and Jean-Michel Poffet, eds., *Jésus de Nazareth: Nouvelles approches d'une énigme* (Geneva: Labor et Fidès, 1998), 225ff. The Gospel of Matthew was composed in an urban context—perhaps Antioch, or, more likely, a city in Palestine, maybe Caesarea—in the years around 80. That of Luke—much more elaborate in its style and conceptual framework—was probably written in Antioch, again in the 80s: E. Earle Ellis, *The Gospel of Luke* (London: Nelson, 1966); Jack Dean Kingsbury, *Matthew: Structure, Christology, Kingdom* (London: S.P.C.K., 1976); Ian Howard Marshall, *The Gospel of Luke* (Exeter, UK: Paternoster Press, 1978); Robert Maddox, *The Purpose of Luke–Acts* (Edinburgh: T. & T. Clark, 1982); Robert H. Gundry, *Matthew: A Commentary on his Literary and Theological Art* (Grand Rapids, MI: William B. Eerdmans, 1982); Joseph A. Fitzmyer, *The Gospel according to Luke*, 2 vols. (Garden City, NY: Doubleday, 1983–85); Eduard Schweizer, *Das Evangelium nach Lucas,* 3rd ed. (Göttingen: Vandenhoeck & Ruprecht, 1986), in English as *The Good News according to Luke,* translated by David E. Green (London: S.P.C.K., 1984); Philip Francis Esler, *Community and Gospel in Luke–Acts: The Social and Political Motivations of Lucan Theology* (Cambridge, UK: Cambridge University Press, 1987); Alan F. Segal, "Matthew's Jewish Voice," in David L. Balch, ed., *Social History of the Matthean Community: Cross Disciplinary Approaches* (Minneapolis: Fortress Press, 1991), 3ff.

The narrative structure of the Gospel of John, on the other hand, is very different, so much so as to prompt the now classic formulation "Either the Synoptics, or John": see the prologue and chapter 1. It was probably written for a Christian community that split away from Judaism—in Alexandria, Antioch, or Ephesus (the most reliable hypothesis)—between 85 and 95. Martin Hengel, *Die johanneische Frage* (Tübingen: Mohr, 1993), preceded by the English edition, *The Johannine Question* (London: SCM Press, 1989), is a very fine and useful book. Oscar Cullmann, *Der Johanneische Kreis: sein Platz im Spätjudentum, im der Jüngerschaft und im Urchristentum: Zum Ursprung des Johannesevangeliums* (Tübingen: Mohr, 1975), in English as *The Johannine Circle: Its Place in Judaism, among the Disciples of Jesus and in Early Christianity: A Study in the Origin of the Gospel of John,* translated by John Bowden (London: SCM Press, 1976), is also a stimulating study, as are all this author's works. Also to be taken into consideration: Charles Harold Dodd, *Historical Tradition in the Fourth Gospel* (Cambridge, UK: Cambridge University Press, 1963); David Resenberger, "The Politics of John: The Trial of Jesus in the Fourth Gospel," *Journal of Biblical Literature* 103 (1984): 395ff.; Barnabas Lindars, *The Gospel of John* (London: Oliphants, 1972), but see also Id., *Essays on John,* edited by C. M. Tuckett (Leuven: Peeters, 1992); Charles K. Barrett, *The Gospel according to St. John: An Introduction with Commentary and Notes on the Greek Text,* 2nd ed. (Philadelphia: Westminster, 1978); Raymond E. Brown, *The Gospel according to John,* 2 vols. (Garden City, NY: Doubleday, 1966–70); R. Alan Culpepper, *Anatomy of the Fourth Gospel: A Study in Literary Design* (Philadelphia: Fortress Press, 1983); John Ashton, *Understanding the Fourth Gospel* (Oxford: Oxford University Press, 1991).

For all the Greek New Testament texts (Gospels and Paul) I followed the Merk edition, *Novum Testamentum graece et latine apparatu critico instructum,* 11th ed. (Rome: Pontificio Istituto Biblico, 1992), also compared with the Nestle–Aland edition, 24th ed. (Stuttgart: Deutsche Bibel Gesellschaft, 1961).

For the Greek text of the Old Testament, I followed the Rahlfs edition, 5th ed. (Stuttgart: Privilegierte Wüttembergische Bibel Anstalt, 1952).

The English translations, from both the Old and New Testaments, are taken, unless otherwise specified in the notes, from the New Revised Standard Version, Anglicized text, cross-reference edition, managing editor Martin H. Mansen, consultant editors John Barton and Bruce M. Metzger (Oxford: Oxford University Press, 2003).

For the Apocrypha of the New Testament, I used the now classic edition of Constantin von Tischendorf, *Evangelia Apocrypha,* 2nd ed. (Leipzig: Mendelssohn, 1876), and that of M. R. James, *The Apocryphal New Testament: Being the Apocryphal Gospels, Acts,*

Epistles, and Apocalypses (Oxford: Clarendon Press, 1924). For the Qumran texts, see the notes to chapter 2.

The work by Philo that interests us is the *Legatio ad Gaium*, which I read in the Cohn–Reiter edition, in *Philonis Alexandrini opera quae supersunt*, vol. 6 (Berlin: De Gruyter, reprint 1962), referring also to the Pelletier edition in *Les Ouvres de Philon d'Alexandrie* (Paris: Les Editions du Cerf, 1972). See Daniel R. Schwartz, "Josephus and Philo on Pontius Pilate," *The Jerusalem Cathedra* 3 (1983): 26ff.

The text about Pilate in Tacitus, from the fifteenth book of the *Annals*, is highly controversial: I referred to the Oxford edition of Charles D. Fisher (Oxford: Clarendon Press, 1906) and the Bibliotheca Teubneriana edition of Heinz Heubner (Stuttgart: Teubner, 1983): see the notes to chapter 2, and also Robert E. Van Voorst, *Jesus outside the New Testament: An Introduction to the Ancient Evidence* (Grand Rapids, MI: W. B. Eerdmans, 2000). More straightforward is the passage from Tertullian in *Apologeticum*, for which I used the Waltzig–Severyns edition in the Les Belles Lettres series (Paris: Les Belles Lettres, 2003).

The epigraph bearing the name of Pilate found in Caesarea during an archeological dig conducted by the Accademia di Scienze e Lettere of the Istituto Lombardo, was published for the first time by Antonio Frova, "L'iscrizione di Ponzio Pilato a Cesarea," *Rendiconti dell'Istituto Lombardo: Classe di Lettere e Scienze morali e storiche* 95 (1961): 419ff., and in *L'Année épigraphique*, 1963: 104, and then returned to on various occasions, for example: 1971: 477; 2008: 1542. See: Jerry Vardaman, "A New Inscription which mentions Pilate as 'Prefect'," *Journal of Biblical Literature* 81 (1962): 70–71; J. H. Ganze, *Ecclesia* 174 (1963): 137; Attilio Degrassi,

"Sull'iscrizione di Ponzio Pilato," *Atti dell'Accademia Nazionale dei Lincei,* 8th series, *Classe di scienze morali, storiche e filologiche,* vol. 19 (Rome: 1964), 59ff. (also in Id., "Scritti vari di antichità," vol. 3 [Venice: Società Istriana di Archeologia e Storia Patria, 1967], 269ff.). See also the notes to chapter 2.

II. The Modern Historiography

The bibliography on the themes dealt with in this book is endless. What follows provides just an indication of the works I bore in mind most during the writing of this volume, and which offer useful lines of further inquiry and research for the reader.

It seemed appropriate to divide the references into three distinct sections, corresponding to the main themes tackled: the life and career of Pilate; Roman Judaea; and Pilate's encounter with Jesus (history, politics, theology). The order within each section is chronological.

THE LIFE AND CAREER OF PILATE

The books devoted entirely to Pilate are not great in number. The first genuinely modern monograph produced by an adequately developed historic criticism is that of Gustaf Adolf Müller, *Pontius Pilatus, der fünfte Prokurator von Judäa und Richter Jesu von Nazareth* (Stuttgart: J. B. Metzler, 1888): still of some interest today (despite the dated positivistic frame), with an extensive bibliography going back to the sixteenth century, it is characterized by the author's evident sympathy for the man. This interpretation was subsequently accepted both by Ernst von Dobschütz, "Pilatus," in *Real-Enzyclopädie für protestantische Theologie und Kirche*, vol. 15 (Leipzig: J. C. Hinrichs'sche Buchhandlung, 1904), 397ff., and by Hermann Peter, "Pontius Pilatus, der Römische Landpfleger in Judäa," *Neues Jahrbuch für die klassische Altertum, Geschichte und deutschen Literatur* 19 (1907): 1ff., but not shared by Emil Schürer, *Geschichte des Judischen Volkes im Zeitalter Jesu Christi*, 3 vols. (Leipzig: Hinrich, 1886–1890, 4th. ed. 1901–1911), in English, in a reworked and updated version edited by Géza Vermès, Fergus Millar, and Martin Goodman, as *The History of the Jewish People in the Age of Jesus Christ (175 B.C.–A.D. 135)*, 3 vols. (Edinburgh: T. & T. Clark, 1973–87), vol. 1, 383ff.—a very important study. Müller's stance was also called into question by Ethelbert Stauffer, in a well-known book that has been republished several times, *Christ und die Caesaren: historische Skizzen* (Hamburg: F. Wittig, 1948), in English as *Christ and the Caesars: Historical Sketches*, translated by K. and R. Gregor Smith (London: SCM Press, 1955), 118ff. (but see also Id., "Zur Muenzpraegung und Judenpolitik des Pontius Pilatus," *La Nouvelle Clio* 1–2 [1949–50]: 495ff.); also see Menahem Stern, "The Province of Judea," in Menahem Stern and Shemuel Safrai, eds., *The Jewish People in the First Century: Historical Geography, Political History, Social, Cultural and Religious Life and Institutions*, 2nd. ed., vol. I (Assen: Van Gorcum, 1987), 308ff. (a volume deserving of attention as a whole).

A number of subsequent studies, of no particular pertinence to our reconstruction, are Gustav Lippert, *Pilatus als Richter: Eine Untersuchung über seine richterliche Verantwortlichkeit an der Hand der Evangelien entnommenen amtlichen Aufzeichnung des Verfahrens* gegen Jesus (Vienna: Osterreichischen Staatsdruckerei, 1923); Frank Morison, *And Pilate Said – A New Study of the Roman Procurator* (London: Rich & Cowan, 1939); Erich Fascher, *Das Weib des Pilatus (Matthaeus 27,19), Die Aufwerkung der Heiligen (Matthaeus 27, 51–53): Zwei Studien zur Geschichte der Schriftauslegung* (Halle: M. Niemeyer, 1951); and Paul Luther Maier, *Pontius Pilate* (Garden City, NY: Doubleday, 1968). On the other hand, an important and carefully researched work is Jean-Pierre Lémonon, *Pilate et la gouvernement de la Judée: Textes et monuments* (Paris: Librairie Lecoffre, 1981), on which see also Horst R. Moehring, *Journal of Biblical Literature* 102 (1983): 490–91. Also not to be missed is Helen K. Bond, *Pontius Pilate in History and Interpretation* (Cambridge, UK: Cambridge University Press, 1998, reprint 2000), on which Robert J. Karris, *Journal of Biblical Literature,* 119 (2000): 762ff.; Bond's study, together with that of Lémonon, are two essential points of reference (note also, by this author, Id., *Caiaphas: Friend of Rome and Judge of Jesus?* [Louisville, KY: Westminster John Knox Press, 2004]). Also worthy of note are Ralf-Peter Märtin, *Pontius Pilatus: Römer, Ritter, Richter* (Munich: Piper, 1989), and Massimo Centini, *Ponzio Pilato: storia e leggenda del procuratore romano che crocifisse il Figlio di Dio* (Casale Monferrato: Piemme, 1994). Of some interest, though debatable, is Ann Wroe, *Pilate: The Biography of an Invented Man* (London: Jonathan Cape, 1999). More recent studies worth reading are Karl Jaroš, *In Sachen Pontius Pilatus* (Mainz: Von Zabern, 2002); Warren Carter, *Pontius Pilate: Portraits of a Roman Governor* (Collegeville, MN: Liturgical Press, 2003)—as regards which, consideration should also be given to R. S. Sugirtharajah, *Postcolonial Criticism and Biblical Interpretation* (Oxford: Oxford University

Press, 2002), especially 79ff.; and, above all, Alexander Demandt, *Pontius Pilatus* (Munich: C. H. Beck, 2012)—in addition to an earlier work, Id., *Hände in Unschuld: Pontius Pilatus in der Geschichte* (Cologne: Böhlau, 1999)—and the short book by Giorgio Agamben, *Pilato e Gesù* (Rome: Nottetempo, 2013), in English as *Pilate and Jesus,* translated by Adam Kotsko (Stanford: Stanford University Press, 2015). Finally: the anthology edited by Jean-Marc Vercruysse, *Ponce Pilate* (Arras: Artois Presses Université, 2013).

To these books I must also add an essay that is not strictly speaking a book of history—something between fiction and the interpretation of a character—but which has accompanied me throughout my research, a work dedicated not to Pilate but to Judas: Mario Brelich, *L'opera del tradimento* (1975), 3rd ed. (Rome: Adelphi, 2008).

Pilate was also the focus of at least three great literary reelaborations, in the nineteenth and twentieth centuries: Anatole France's short story "Le procurateur de Judée" (1892), in *Oeuvres,* vol. I (Paris: Pleiade, 1984), 877ff., in English as "The Procurator of Judea," translated by Frederick Chapman, in Konrad Bercovici, ed., *Best Short Stories of the World* (New York: Garden City, 1925); Mikhail Bulgakov's *The Master and Margarita* (finished by his wife in 1941, but only published in 1966–67, and then, in a complete edition, in 1973), which I know from the Italian translation by Maria Olsoufieva (Milan: Garzanti, 1973) and the English one by Michael Glenny (London: Harvill Press, 1967; reprint 1993): Bulgakov had read Müller's monograph, from which he drew inspiration with total liberty and absolute brilliance: three fine essays on this novel, from among many, are Richard W. Pope, "Ambiguity and Meaning in *The Master and Margarita:* The Role of Afranius," *Slavic Review* 36 (1977): 1ff.; Gary Rosenshield, "The *Master and Margarita* and the Poetics of Aporia: A Polemical Article," *Slavic Review* 56 (1997): 187ff., especially 191ff. (though not all his views can be shared); and Susan Amert, "The Dialectics of Closure in Bulgakov's *Master and Margarita,*" *Russian Review* 61 (2002): 599ff.; and finally that of Friedrich Dürrenmatt, *Pilatus* (Olten: Beck, 1949), of the three interpretations, the one I like least. There are bare mentions of Pilate in two fine books: José Saramago, *O Evangelho segundo Jesus Cristo: romance* (Lisbon: Caminho, 1991), in English as *The Gospel according to Jesus Christ,* translated by Giovanni Pontiero (San Diego: Harcourt Brace, 1994); and Emmanuel Carrère, *Le Royaume* (Paris: P. O. L. Editeur, 2014).

Much more abundant are the articles, and encyclopedia and dictionary entries, some of significant importance, on Pilate, or the pages devoted to him in essays about the "trial" of Jesus. For the latter, see the books referred to in the third section of this overview. For the others, we can begin with several now quite old works—some very brief, but which I believe are still worth remembering—on issues addressed in this book: Marie-Joseph Olliver, "Ponce Pilate et les Pontii," *Revue Biblique* 5 (1896): 244ff.; George F. Abbott, "The Report and Death of Pilate," *Journal of Theological Studies* 4 (1903): 83ff.; Martin Dibelius, "Herodes und Pilatus," *Zeitschrift für neutestamentliche Wissenschaft* 19 (1915): 113ff.; Urban Holzmeister, "Wann war Pilatus Prokurator von Judaea?" *Biblica* 13 (1932): 228ff.; P. L. Hadley, "Pilate's Arrival in Judaea," *Journal of Theological Studies* 35 (1934): 56–57; Sigfried Jan de Laet, "Le successeur de Ponce Pilate," *L'Antiquité Classique* 8

(1939): 413ff.; Antony D. Doyle, "Pilate's Career and the Date of the Crucifixion," *Journal of Theological Studies* 42 (1941): 190ff.; Carl H. Kraeling, "The Episode of the Roman Standards at Jerusalem," *Harvard Theological Review* 35 (1942): 263ff.; Stephen Liberty, "The Importance of Pontius Pilate in Creed and Gospel," *Journal of Theological Studies* 45 (1944): 18ff.

From the 1950s onward the number of works—mostly brief notes—multiplies, and I can only indicate a limited selection here: E. Mary Smallwood, "The Date of the Dismissal of Pontius Pilate from Judaea," *Journal of Jewish Studies* 5 (1954): 12ff.; Josef Blinzler, "Der Entscheid des Pilatus: Executionsbefehl oder Todesurteil?," *Münchener Theologische Zeitschrift* 5 (1954): 171ff.; Salvatore Garofalo, "L'imprevedibile carriera di Ponzio Pilato," *Historia* 2 (1958): 12ff.; Ernst Haenchen, "Jesus vor Pilatus (Joh.18,28–19,15)," *Theologische Literaturzeitung* 85 (1960): 93ff.; Paul Winter, "A Letter from Pontius Pilate," *Novum Testamentum* 7 (1964): 37ff. (a pleasing divertissement: a much more important work by this author will be referred to later on, in the final section of this overview); Alois Bajsic, "Pilatus, Jesus and Barabba," *Biblica* 48 (1967): 7ff.; S. G. F. Brandon, "Pontius Pilate in History and Legend," *History Today* 18 (1968): 525ff.; Paul L. Maier, "Sejanus, Pilate, and the Date of the Crucifixion," *Church History* 37 (1968): 3ff.; Id., "The Episode of the Golden Roman Shields at Jerusalem," *Harvard Theological Review* 62 (1969): 109ff.; John F. Quinn, "The Pilate Sequence in the Gospel of Matthew," *Dunwoodie Review* 10 (1970): 154ff (an interesting work); J. E. Allen, "Why Pilate?" in Ernst Bammel, ed., *Trial of Jesus: Cambridge Studies in Honor of C. F. D. Moule* (London: SCM Press, 1970): 78ff. (which will also be cited in section 3 below);

Harold W. Hoenher, "Why Did Pilate Hand Jesus Over to Antipas?," in Bammel, ed., *Trial of Jesus,* 84ff.; Brian C. McGing, "Pontius Pilate and the Sources," *Catholic Biblical Quarterly* 53 (1991): 416ff. (a useful synthesis); Daniel R. Schwartz, "Pontius Pilate's Appointment to Office and the Chronology of Josephus' *Antiquities,* Books 18–20," in *Studies in the Jewish Background of Christianity* (Tübingen: Mohr, 1992), 182ff.; Klaus-Stephan Krieger, "Pontius Pilate: ein Judenfriend? Zur Problematik einer Pilatusbiographie," *Biblische Notitien* 78 (1995): 63ff.; Joan E. Taylor, "Pontius Pilate and the Imperial Cult in Roman Judaea," *New Testament Studies* 52 (2006): 555ff.

In addition, a number of entries on Pilate in encyclopedias, lexicons, and dictionaries, again almost invariably very brief: George T. Purves, in James Hastings, ed., *Dictionary of the Bible,* vol. 3 (Edinburgh: T. & T. Clark, and New York: Charles Scribner's Sons, 1900), 875ff.; Alexander Souter, in James Hastings, ed., *Dictionary of Christ and the Gospels,* vol. 2 (Edinburgh: T. & T. Clark, 1908), 363ff.; E. Fascher, in *Pauly-Wissowa Real-Encyclopädie der classischen Altertumwissenschaft,* vol. 20 (Stuttgart: J. B. Metzler, 1950), coll. 1322f.; Ernst Bammel, in *Religion in Geschichte und Gegenwart,* vol. 5, 3rd ed. (Tübingen: Mohr, 1961), 383–84; Samuel Sandmel, in *The Interpreters' Dictionary of the Bible,* vol. 3 (Nashville: Abingdon Press, 1962), 811ff.; Josef Blinzler, in *Lexicon für Theologie und Kirche,* vol. 8 (Freiburg: Herder Verlag, 1963), 504–5; Albert Ernest Hillard and Henri Clavier, in James Hastings, ed., *Dictionary of the Bible,* 2nd edition (Edinburgh: T. & T. Clark, 1963), 771–72; F. J. Buckley, in *New Catholic Encyclopaedia,* vol. 11 (New York: McGraw-Hill: 1967), 360–61; L. Roth, in *Encyclopaedia Judaica,* vol. 13 (New York:

Macmillan, 1971), 848; Harold W. Hoehner, in *Dictionary of Jesus and the Gospels* (Downers Grove, IL: InterVarsity Press, 1992), 616.

Of importance, finally, in reconstructing Pilate's career, are: Hans-Georg Pflaum, *Les procurateurs équestre sous le Haut-Empire romain* (Paris: Adrien Maisonneuve, 1950), and Id., *Le carrières procuratoriennes équestre sous le Haut-Empire romain*, vol. 3 (Paris: P. Geuthner, 1961), 1082; Ségolène Demougin, *L'ordre équestre sous les Julio-Claudiens* (Rome: École Française de Rome, 1988), especially 275ff., 323ff., 712ff., 830, and Id., *Prosopographie des chevaliers romains Julio-Claudiens (43 av. J-C.–70 ap. J-C)* (Rome: École Française de Rome, 1992), 17, 246–47; Rudolf Haensch, *Capita provinciarum: Statthaltersitze und Provinzialverwaltung in der roemischen Kaiserzeit* (Mainz: Philipp von Zabern, 1997), 227ff.; Andreina Magioncalda, "I governatori delle province procuratorie: carriere," in Ségolène Demougin, Hubert Devijver, and Marie-Thérèse Raepsaet-Charlier, eds., *L'Ordre équestre: Histoire d'une aristocratie (IIe siècle av. J.-C. – IIIe siècle ap. J.-C.)* (Rome: École Française de Rome, 1999), 391ff. See also Davide Faoro, *Praefectus, procurator, praeses: Genesi delle cariche presidiali equestri nell'Alto Impero Romano* (Milan: Le Monnier, 2011), 10, 72, 88–89, 94, 105, 112, 114ff., 137ff.

ROMAN JUDAEA

We must begin with two essential works: Fergus Millar, *The Roman Near East: 31 BC–AD 337* (Cambridge, MA: Harvard University Press, 1993; 4th ed., 2001), especially 337ff.; and Maurice Sartre, *D'Alexandre à Zénobie: Histoire du Levant antique IV siècle av. J.-C. – III siècle ap. J.-C.* (Paris: Fayard, 2001), 305ff., 337ff., 383ff., 530ff. Immediately after these, we should consider: A. H. M.

Jones, *Studies in Roman Government and Law* (Oxford: Basil Blackwell, 1968), 115ff.; E. Mary Smallwood, *The Jews under Roman Rule: From Pompey to Diocletian* (Leiden: Brill, 1976), especially 144ff. and 160ff. (but see also Id., "Some Notes on the Jews under Tiberius," *Latomus* 15 [1956]: 314ff.; Id., "High Priests and Politics in Roman Palestine," *Journal of Theological Studies* 13 [1962]: 14ff.; Id., "Behind the New Testament," *Greece and Rome,* 2nd series, 17 [1970]: 81ff.), and a youthful study by Arnaldo Momigliano, precious but little quoted, entitled "Ricerche sull'organizzazione della Giudea sotto il dominio romano (63 a.C.-70 d.C)," in *Annali della R. Scuola Normale Superiore di Pisa,* series 2, vol. 3 (1934, reprint Amsterdam: Adolf M. Hakkert, 1967), which I cite. The essay is now also in Id., *Nono contributo alla storia dei studi classici ed del mondo antico,* edited by Riccardo di Donato (Rome: Edizioni di storia ed letteratura, 1992), 227ff. An overall picture full of interesting ideas can be found in the very recent work of Simon Schama, *The Story of the Jews: Finding the Words. 1000 BC–1492 AD* (New York: HarperCollins, 2013), 88ff., 173ff. (discussed by Glen W. Bowersock, *New York Review of Books* 61, no. 7 [April 24, 2014]: 41ff.); and in Mario Liverani, *Oltre la Bibbia: Storia antica di Israele* (Bari: Laterza, 2003), 223ff., 275ff., in English as *Israel's History and the History of Israel,* translated by Chiara Peri and Philip R. Davies (Abingdon, UK, and New York: Routledge, 2014), 203ff., 250ff., even if it does not specifically deal with the historical period considered in this book. Likewise to be considered: Emilio Gabba, "The Social, Economic and Political History of Palestine 63 BCE–70 CE," in William Horbury, W. D. Davies, and John Sturdy, eds., *The Cambridge History of Judaism,* vol. 3, *The Early Roman Period* (Cambridge, UK:

Cambridge University Press, 1999), 94ff.; Andrea Giardina, Mario Liverani, and Biancamaria Scarcia, *La Palestina* (Rome: Editori Riuniti, 1987), 73ff.; Israel Shatzman, "L'integrazione della Giudea nell'impero romano," in Ariel Lewin, ed., *Gli ebrei nell'impero romano: Saggi vari* (Florence: Giuntina, 2001), 17ff.; Valerio Marotta, "Conflitti politici e governo provinciale," in Francesco Amarelli, ed., *Politica e partecipazione nelle città dell'impero romano* (Rome: L'Erma di Bretschneider, 2005), 121ff.

Also deserving of attention: Ian H. Eybers, "The Roman Administration of Judaea between AD 6 and 41, with special reference to the procuratorship of Pontius Pilate," *Theologica Evangelica* 2 (1969): 131ff.; Daniela Piattelli, "Ricerche intorno alle relazioni politiche tra Roma e l'*ethnos ton Ioydaion* dall 161 a.C. all'4 a.C.," *Bullettino dell'Istituto di Diritto Romano "Vittorio Scialoja"* 74 (1971): 219ff.; Michael Grant, *The Jews in the Roman World* (London: Weidenfeld & Nicolson, 1973); Shemuel Safrai, "Jewish Self-Government", in Safrai and Stern, eds., *The Jewish People,* 337ff.; Glen B. Bowersock, "Old and New in the History of Judaea," *Journal of Roman Studies* 65 (1975): 180ff. (an important review of the book by Schürer already cited, *Geschichte des Judischen Volkes im Zeitalter Jesu Christi*); Shimon Applebaum, "Judea as a Roman Province: The Countryside as a Political and Economic Factor," *Aufstieg und Niedergang der roemischen Welt* 11, no. 8 (1977): 355ff.; John R. Bartlett, *Jews in the Hellenistic World. Josephus, Aristeas, the Sibylline Oracles, Eupolemus* (Cambridge, UK: Cambridge University Press, 1985); Martin Goodman, *The Ruling Class of Judaea: The Origins of the Jewish Revolt against Rome, AD 66–70* (Cambridge, UK: Cambridge University Press, 1987); Anthony J. Saldarini,

Pharisees, Scribes and Sadducees in Palestinian Society: A Sociological Approach (Edinburgh: T. & T. Clark, 1989); Giulio Firpo, "I Giudei," in Aldo Schiavone, ed., *Storia di Roma*, vol. 2.2 (Turin: Einaudi, 1991), 527ff. (also worth remembering in this volume is the essay by Glen W. Bowersock, "La Grecia e le province orientali," 409ff). Also useful, finally, is Benjamin Isaac and Yuval Shahar, *Judaea-Palestina, Babylon and Rome: Jews in Antiquity: Texts and Studies in Ancient Judaism* (Tübingen: Mohr, 2012), and Simon Claude Mimouni, *Le Judaïsme anciens du VIe siècle avant notre ère au IIIe siècle de notre ère: des prêtres aux rabbins* (Paris: Presses Universitaires de France, 2012), 415ff.

A picture of the city of Jerusalem in the Roman age can be found in Simon Sebag Montefiore, *Jerusalem: The Biography* (London: Phoenix, 2011, reprint 2012), 86ff. Essential reading is Joachim Jeremias, *Jerusalem in the Time of Jesus: An Investigation into Economic and Social Conditions during the New Testament Period* (London: SCM Press, 1969). Also worth reading: John Wilkinson, "Ancient Jerusalem: Its Water Supply and Population," *Palestine Exploration Quarterly* 106 (1974): 33ff.; Magen Broshi, "La population de l'ancienne Jérusalem," *Revue Biblique* 82 (1975): 5ff.; Baruch Lifshitz, "Jérusalem sous la domination romaine: Histoire de la ville depuis la conquête de Pompée jusqu'à Constantin (63a.C–325 p.C)," *Aufstieg und Niedergang Der Römischen Welt* II, no. 8 (1977): 444ff.

For the cultural history of Judaea from the Hasmonean age to the first century, and on the relations with the Hellenistic tradition, two works that cannot be disregarded are Martin Hengel, *Judaism and Hellenism: Studies in their Encounter in Pales-*

tine during the Early Hellenistic Period, 2 vols., 2nd ed., translated by John Bowden (Philadelphia: Fortress Press, 1974)—on which, see Fergus Millar, "The Background to the Maccabean Revolution: Reflections on Martin Hengel's *Judaism and Hellenism,*" *Journal of Jewish Studies* 29 (1978): 1ff.—and Id., *The 'Hellenization' of Judaea in the First Century after Christ* (London: SCM Press, 1989); also worthy of consideration by this author is Id., *Between Jesus and Paul: Studies in the Earliest History of Christianity,* translated by John Bowden (London: SCM Press, 1983). Another work that remains important is: Arnaldo Momigliano, *Alien Wisdom: The Limits of Hellenization* (Cambridge, UK: Cambridge University Press, 1975), especially 97ff. See also: Marcel Simon, *Les Sectes juives au temps de Jésus* (Paris: Presses Universitaires de France, 1960), in English as *Jewish Sects at the Time of Jesus,* translated by James H. Farley (Philadelphia: Fortress Press, 1967); A. N. Sherwin White, *Roman Society and Roman Law in the New Testament* (Oxford: Clarendon Press, 1963)—an important book; Louis H. Feldman, "How Much Hellenism in Jewish Palestine?," *Hebrew Union College Annual* 57 (1986): 83 ff., and then Id., *Studies in Hellenistic Judaism* (Leiden: Brill, 1996); and E. P. Sanders, *Judaism: Practice and Belief: 63 BCE–66 CE* (London: SCM Press, 1992).

PILATE'S ENCOUNTER WITH JESUS

It is impossible to give a full bibliography on the "trial" of Jesus—I prefer to talk of Pilate's "investigation" of Jesus—and of his condemnation. In this sea of writing, I have kept two works firmly in mind throughout the course of my research: Josef Blinzler, *Der Prozess Jesu: Vierte, emeut revidierte Auflage,* 1951, 3rd. ed. (Regensburg: Verlag Friedrich Pustet, 1969), in English as *The Trial of Jesus*, translated by Isabel and Florence McHugh (Westminster, MD: Newman Press, 1959; the translation is based on the second edition); and Haim H. Cohn, *The Trial and Death of Jesus* (New York: Harper & Row, 1971), of which a first version, in Hebrew, appeared in 1968. Besides these books, I also consider of great importance the work of Fergus Millar, "Reflections on the Trial of Jesus," in Philip R. Davies and Richard T. White, eds., *A Tribute to Geza Vermes: Essays on Jewish and Christian Literature and History* (Sheffield, UK: JSOT Press, 1990), 355ff. Three other works that stand out are Paul Winter, *On the Trial of Jesus* (Berlin: De Gruyten, 1961), 2nd ed., revised and edited by T. A. Burkill and Geza Vermes (Berlin: Gruyter, 1974), on which see Solomon Zeitlin, "The Trial of Jesus," *Jewish Quarterly Review* 53 (1962): 78ff; S. G. F. Brandon, *The Trial of Jesus of Nazareth* (London: Batsford, 1968); and, above all, Raymond E. Brown, *The Death of the Messiah: From Gethsemane to the Grave: A Commentary on the Passion Narratives in the Four Gospels*, 2 vols. (New York: Doubleday, 1994). An excellent overall picture emerges from the first three chapters of Charles Freeman, *A New History of Early Christianity* (New Haven: Yale University Press, 2009), and in Francesco Amarelli and Francesco Lucrezi, eds., *Il processo contro Gesù* (Naples: Jovene, 1999).

Also worth consulting are: Simon Légasse, *The Trial of Jesus* (London: SCM Press, 1997), and two earlier works, T. A. Burkill, "The Trial of Jesus," *Vigiliae Christianae* 12 (1958): 1ff., and Paul W. Walasky, "The Trial and Death of Jesus in the Gospel of Luke," *Journal of Biblical Literature* 94 (1975): 81ff. Of continuing importance are the considerations of A. N. Sherwin White, *Roman Soci-*

ety and Roman Law in the New Testament (Oxford: Clarendon Press, 1963), especially 24ff. (on which T. A. Burkill, "The Condemnation of Jesus: a critique of Sherwin White's Thesis," *Novum Testamentum* 12 [1970]: 321ff.).

For the theological issues that emerge during Pilate's inquiry, I particularly bore in mind the works of Jan Assmann: *Herrschaft und Heil: Politische Theologie in Altaegypten, Israel, und Europa* (Munich: Carl Hanser Verlag, 2000), *Monotheismus und die Sprache der Gewalt* (Vienna: Picus, 2006), *Die Mosaische Unterscheidung oder der Preis des Monotheismus* (Munich: Carl Hanser Verlag, 2003), in English as *The Price of Monotheism,* translated by Robert Savage (Stanford: Stanford University Press, 2010), *Of God and Gods: Egypt, Israel and the Rise of Monotheism* (Madison: University of Wisconsin Press, 2008); and the interpretations of Carl Schmitt, *Politische Theologie: Vier Kapitel zur Lehre von der Souveranitaet* (Munich: Duncker & Humblot, 1922), in English as *Political Theology: Four Chapters on the Concept of Sovereignty,* translated by George Schwab (Cambridge, MA: MIT Press, 1985), and *Politische Theologie II: Die Legende von der Erledigung jeder politischen Theologie* (Berlin: Duncker & Humblot, 1970), in English as *Political Theology II: The Myth of the Closure of any Political Theology,* translated by Michael Hoetzl and Graham Ward (Cambridge, UK: Polity, 2008); of Erik Peterson, "Was ist Theologie" (1925), now in *Ausgewaelte Schriften,* vol. 1, *Theologische Traktate* (Wuerzburg: Echter, 1994), and "Der Monotheismus als politisches Problem" (1935), now also in *Ausgewaelte Schriften*; of Jacob Taubes, *Die politische Theologie des Paulus* (Munich: Wilhelm Fink, 1993), in English as *The Political Theology of Paul,* translated by Dana Hollander, edited by Aleida and Jan Assmann (Stanford:

Stanford University Press, 2004), and "Theology and Political Theory," *Social Research* 22 (1955): 57ff.; and of Roberto Esposito, *Due: La macchina della teologia politica e il posto del pensiero* (Turin: Einaudi, 2013), in English as *Two. The Machine of Political Theology and the Place of Thought*, translated by Zakiya Hanafi (New York: Fordham University Press, 2015), a book rich in doctrine and ideas. I also took great account of Ernst Kantorowicz, *The King's Two Bodies: A Study in Medieval Political Theology* (Princeton: Princeton University Press, 1957)—a genuine masterpiece. Other references can be found in the notes to chapters 3 and 4.

NOTES

✝

A number of texts in the Notes are listed with the short-title format only. In these cases, full bibliographic details can be found in Sources and Historiography.

INTRODUCTION

11   "history and memory": Jan Assmann, *Das kulturelle Gedächtnis: Schrift, Erinnerung und politiche Identität im frühen Hochkulturen* (Munich: C. H. Beck, 1992); and Id., *Moses the Egyptian: The Memory of Egypt in Western Monotheism* (Cambridge, MA: Harvard University Press, 1997).

12   "Augustine": Saint Augustine, *In Evangelium Joannis Tractatus* (J.-P. Migne, *Patrologia Latina*, vol. 35), 115–17, in English as *Lectures or Tractates on the Gospel according to St. John,* translated by John Gibb (Edinburgh: T & T Clark, 1873; reprint 1983).

12   "It has been authoritatively shown": By Fergus Millar in "Reflections on the Trial of Jesus," 359.

1. ONE NIGHT IN THE MONTH OF NISAN

19   "Caesarea": Robert J. Bull, "Césarée Maritime," *Revue Biblique* 82 (1975): 278ff.; Lee I. Levine, *Roman Caesarea: An Archaeological–Topographical Study* (Jerusalem: Institute of Archaeology, Hebrew University of Jerusalem, 1975).

19 "furnished and ready": Mk 14:15; Lk 22:12.

20 "One tradition": Attributed to Epiphanius, bishop of Salamis, who died in 403.

20 "Jerusalem": Sartre, *D'Alexandre à Zénobie*, 312; Broshi, "La population de l'ancienne Jérusalem," 5ff.; Wilkinson, "Ancient Jerusalem: Its Water Supply and Population," 33ff.; Lémonon, *Pilate et la gouvernement de la Judée*, 117ff.

20 "complicated, even astronomical, calculations": John K. Fotheringham, "The Evidence of Astronomy and Technical Chronology for the Date of the Crucifixion," *Journal of Theological Studies* 35 (1934): 146ff. I accept the date sustained by Josef Blinzler in *The Trial of Jesus*, 72ff., and by many others he cites. Millar, "Reflections," 355 and 380, note 1, finds convincing the arguments of Nikkos Kokkinos, "Crucifixion in AD 36: the Keystone for Dating the Birth of Jesus," in Jerry Vardaman and Edwin M. Yamauchi, eds., *Chronos, Kairos, Christos: Nativity and Chronological Studies Presented to Jack Finegan* (Winona Lake, IN: Eisenbrauns, 1989), 133—but such a late dating seems entirely implausible. The date of 33 was accepted by Paul Luther Maier in "Sejanus, Pilate and the Date of the Crucifixion," 3ff., with serious but not wholly convincing arguments.

21 "So the population swelled": Between 125,000 and 180,000 visitors, in the hypothesis, which seems reasonable to me, of Alfredo Mordechai Rabello, "E Gesù venne in Gerusalemme ed entrò nel Tempio," in Amarelli and Lucrezi, eds., *Il processo contro Gesù*, 55. On the other hand, the figure reported by Josephus, *Wars*, 6:423–26, is implausible.

23 "Unlike the nearby province of Syria": Michael P. Speidel, "The Roman Army in Judea under the Procurators: The Italian and the Augustan Cohort in the Acts of the Apostles," in *Roman Army Studies*, vol. 2 (Stuttgart: Franz Steiner, 1992), 224ff.; Edward Dabrowa, "The Commanders of Syrian Legions I–III c. AD," in David L. Kennedy, ed., *The Roman Army in the East* (Ann Arbor, MI: Journal of Roman Archaeology, 1996), 277ff., and Id., *Legio X Fretensis: A Prosopographical Study of its Officers* (Stuttgart: Franz Steiner, 1993); also Sartre, *D'Alexandre à Zénobie*, 480ff.

24 "gone up to Jerusalem": Jn 11:55; but also Lk 10:28.

24 "greeted and acclaimed": Jn 12:12–28; Lk 19:29–39, and Mk 11:1–10, are less explicit; Mt 21:1–11 is clearer.

26 "writes Mark": Mk 11:18.

26 "Matthew says": Mt 21:10–11.

26 "we read in Luke": Lk 20:19 (my translation). See also 19:47–48: "The chief priests, the scribes, and the leaders of the people kept looking for a way to

kill him; but they did not find anything they could do, for all the people were spellbound by what they heard."

27 "as John says": Jn 17:1; see also 13:31—the verb is *doxázo*.

27 "The hour . . . has come": Jn 16:32. On Jesus's doubts, I consider the analysis of Mario Brelich, in *L'opera del tradimento*, to be without equal.

27 "writes Luke": Lk 22:41.

28 "distressed and agitated": Mk 14:33—*ekthambeîsthai kaì ademoneîn*.

28 "I am deeply grieved": Mt 26:38.

28 "Luke tells us": Lk 22:44.

28 "Father, if you are willing": Lk 22:42; Mt 26:39; Mk 14:36.

29 "much disputed by historians": It is denied, for example, by Blinzler, *The Trial*, 49ff., but lies at the center of the reconstruction by Cohn in *The Trial and Death of Jesus*, 71ff. The presence of the Romans seems to be accepted by Millar, "Reflections," 370.

30 "an ambiguous sentence in John": Jn 18:12: "The cohort, the tribune, and the Jewish guards took Jesus and bound him." The Roman presence had been mentioned in 18:3.

32 "as has been argued": For example, by Cohn, *Trial*, 86ff.

33 "the extreme idea": Again, of Cohn, *Trial*, 89ff.

33 "according to the Gospels": Mk 14:10–11, 18–20, 43–45; Mt 26:21–23 and 46–50, 27:3–5; Lk 22:3–6, 21:47–48; Jn 13:2–3 (but there is a difficulty in the text), 21:27–29, and 18:2–5. In Mk 14:43, Mt 26:47, and Lk 22:47 reference is made to the presence of a "crowd" (*óchlos* in all three cases), but it is evident that there were only the Temple guards and the Roman soldiers. I will return below to the use of this word in the Synoptics, with regard to the condemnation of Jesus: see notes to chapters 3 and 4.

34 "went to the priests": Mk 14:10–11.

34 "records John": Jn 13:27.

35 "in John's account": Jn 18:4–9.

36 "writes John": Jn 18:10.

36 "Luke does not explain": Lk 22:49–51, where the author of the action is not indicated.

36 "In Matthew and John": Mt 26:51–52 (no name is indicated here either), Jn 18:10–11 (also with the name of the servant who is struck, Malchus).

36 "Have you come out . . . ?": Lk 22:52, Mt 26:55, Mk 14:48.

37 "as John recounts": Jn 18:13.

37   "Josephus": *Antiquities*, 20:198; see also 18:27 and 34.

38   "His residence": Bond, *Caiaphas*, 154ff.

39   "by the seventeenth century": David R. Catchpole, *The Trial of Jesus: A Study in the Gospels and Jewish Historiography from 1770 to the Present Day* (Leiden: Brill, 1971). An essential book is Anton Balthasar von Walther, *Juristisch-historische Betrachtungen über das Leyden und Sterben Jesu Christi: Darinnen Die merckwürdigsten von den vier Evangleistein beschriebne Umstände dieser Geschichte Aus den Römischen wie auch Jüdischen Rechten und Alterthümern erläutet werd* (Breslau: Pietsch, 1738).

39   "mentioned by Josephus": 8:35 and 95.

40   "as John recalls": Jn 11:47–53.

40   "the description of Josephus": See Hugo Mantel, *Studies in the History of the Sanhedrin* (Cambridge, MA: Harvard University Press, 1965).

41   "John's account": Jn 18:13–27.

41   "Luke describes": Lk 22:66–71.

41   "Matthew reports": Mt 26:59–68, 27:1–2.

41   "Even Mark's version": Mk 14:53–65.

42   "He was blindfolded": Lk 22:63.

43   "Spoken of only by John": Jn 18:13–14, 19–24.

44   "Jesus responds memorably": Jn 18:20–21.

45   "Is that how you answer . . . ?": Jn 18:22.

45   "If I have spoken wrongly": Jn 18:23.

47   "Luke's account": Lk 22:67–70.

48   "What further testimony . . . ?": Lk 22:71.

48   "Many": Mk 14:56.

49   "At last two came forward": Mt 26:60.

50   "I put you under oath": Mt 26:63–66.

51   "Bulgakov's brilliant imagining": Mikhail Bulgakov, *The Master and Margarita*, translated by Michael Glenny.

2. ROMAN JUDAEA AND THE WORK OF
THE FIFTH PREFECT

52   "Pilate was in Judaea . . . from the year 26": Different dates, for example 19, are unconvincing. I am in agreement with Bond, *Pontius Pilate in History and Interpretation*, 1, note 1.

53   "Epigraphs dating": Attilio Degrassi, *Inscriptiones Latinae liberae rei publicae*,
      vols. 1–2 (Florence: La Nuova Italia, 1965), for example nos. 231, 515, 524, 772,
      775, 943. See also Ronald Syme, "Personal Names in *Annales* I–VI," in Id., *Ten
      Studies in Tacitus* (Oxford: Clarendon Press, 1970), 71.

53   *"concordia ordinum"*: Cicero, *pro Cluentio*, 55:152; *De coniuratione Catilinae*, 4:15;
      ad Atticum, 1:17:10, 1:17:8, 1:18:3; 2:3:4. Hermann Strasburger, *Concordia ordi-
      num* (Leipzig: R. Noske, 1931), 12ff. and 31ff., is a classic.

54   "the administration of the provinces": Three very different books, which
      together represent an excellent point of departure, are: Francesco De
      Martino, *Storia della costituzione romana*, 2nd ed., vol. 4,2 (Naples: Jovene,
      1975); Fergus Millar, *The Emperor in the Roman World (31 BC–AD 337)*
      (Ithaca, NY: Cornell University Press, 1977; reprint 1992); and Glen W.
      Bowersock, *Augustus and the Greek World* (Oxford: Clarendon Press, 1965;
      reprint 1966).

55   "as Strabo": *Geography*, 17:3:25 (839–40C.).

56   "as Josephus diligently records": *Antiquities*, 18:31–35.

58   "Tacitus mentions it briefly": *Annales*, 2:85:4. Also: Philo, *Legatio ad Gaium*,
      160; Josephus, *Antiquities*, 18:83–84; Suetonius, *Tiberius*, 36.

59   "Philo seems to believe it": *Legatio ad Gaium*, 159–60.

59   "have long divided scholars": Already discussed by Momigliano, "Ricerche
      sull'organizzazione della Giudea sotto il dominio romano (63 a.C.–70 d.C),"
      77.

61   "Some late testimony from Ulpian": 15 *Ad edictum*, in *Digesta* 1.17.1: Orazio
      Licandro, "La prefettura d'Egitto fra conservazione e innovazione istituzi-
      onale," in *Studi per Giovanni Nicosia*, vol. 4 (Milan: Giuffrè Editore, 2007),
      387ff.

61   "Josephus, in the *Antiquities*": *Antiquities*, 18:2: *te epì pasin exousia; Wars*,
      2:117. Particular attention should be given, also regarding what will be
      said later, to Bernardo Santalucia, "'Lo portarono via e lo consegnarono
      al governatore Ponzio Pilato' (Matth, 27,2): la giurisdizione del prefetto
      di Giudea," in Amarelli and Lucrezi, eds., *Il processo contro Gesù*, 87ff.; and
      Id., *Diritto e processo penale nell'antica Roma*, 2nd ed. (Milan: Giuffrè Edi-
      tore, 1998), 183ff. In addition, bear in mind Cristina Giachi, "Un brano
      della traduzione russa del Bellum Judaicum di Flavio Giuseppe e i rapporti
      fra il sinedrio e il governatore romano nel I secolo," in Dario Mantovani
      and Luigi Pellecchi, eds., *Eparcheia, antomonia e civitas Romana: Studi sulla*

    giurisdizione criminale dei governatori di provincia (II sec. a.C.–II d.C) (Pavia: IUSS Press, 2010), 89ff.

63   "Horace had written": *Carmina*, 3:4:65.

64   "Ulpian": Ulp. 7 *De officio proconsulis*, in *Digesta* 1.18.13 pr. See Dario Mantovani, "Il 'bonus praeses' secondo Ulpiano: Studi su contenuto e forma del 'De officio proconsulis' di Ulpiano," *Bullettino dell'Istituto di Diritto Romano Vittorio Scialoja* 96–97 (1993–94): 203ff.

65   *"suis moribus legibusque suis uti"*: reported by Aulus Gellius, *Noctes Atticae*, 16:13:4. See Francesco Grelle, *L'autonomia cittadina fra Traiano e Adriano* (Naples: Edizioni Scientifiche Italiane, 1972), 65ff.

66   "in Cicero's time": I am thinking of Cicero, *Ad Quintum Fratrem*, 1:1:27–28: Aldo Schiavone, *Ius: L'invenzione del diritto in Occidente* (Turin: Einaudi, 2005), in English as *The Invention of Law in the West*, translated by Jeremy Carden and Antony Shugaar (Cambridge, MA: Harvard University Press, 2012), 298ff.

67   "Posidonius": Momigliano, *Alien Wisdom*, 22ff., especially 32ff.

67   "imagined and remembered": my reconstruction takes account of Liverani, *Oltre la Bibbia*; and, naturally, of Assmann, *Herrschaft und Heil* which I consulted in the Italian edition, *Potere e salvezza. Teologia politica nell'antico Egitto, in Israele e in Europe*, translated by Umberto Gandini (Turin: Einaudi, 2002), 40ff., 186ff.; Id., *The Price of Monotheism*, 1ff. and 31ff.; and Id., *Of God and Gods. Egypt, Israel and the Rise of Monotheism* (Madison: University of Wisconsin Press, 2008), consulted in the Italian edition, *Dio e gli dei. Egitto, Israele e la nascita del monoteismo*, translated by L. Santi (Bologna: Il Mulino, 2009), 17ff., 111ff. The concept of the "axial period" (*achsenzeit*), drawn from Assmann and which I presuppose, was developed by Karl Jaspers, *Vom Ursprung und Ziel der Geschichte* (Zurich: Artemis, 1949), in English as *The Origin and the Goal of History*, translated by Michael Bullock (New Haven: Yale University Press, 1953), 1ff.

69   "despite much important research": I am thinking above all of the work of Hengel, *Judaism and Hellenism*.

70   "alien wisdom": the title of the book by Momigliano just cited.

71   "writes Josephus": *Antiquities*, 14:77–78.

71   "in the Psalms of Solomon": 2:26–27. The Psalms are an apocryphal text of the Old Testament, probably composed at the end of the first century BC: their Greek suggests a Hebrew original. I am drawing here on the Holm-

Nielsen edition, *Die Psalmen Salomos* (Gütersloh: Gütersloher Verlagshaus Gerd Mohn, 1977), 66.

75 "as Josephus called them": *Antiquities*, 18:2, and see also *Wars*, 2:119.

75 "According to Josephus": *Wars*, 2:119–66; *Antiquities*, 18:11–25.

76 "writes Luke": Lk 11:39. It is Jesus who is speaking.

76 "they turn aside": *Wars*, 2:120 and 122.

77 "the Qumran sect": Geza Vermes, *The Dead Sea Scolls: Qumran in Perspective* (Cleveland: Collins World, 1978); Florentino García Martínez, *The Dead Sea Scrolls Translated: The Qumran Texts in English* (Leiden: Brill, 1994)—the version to which I refer.

77 "a literature of combat": Sartre, *D'Alexandre à Zénobie*, 367ff.

78 "an obscure pronouncement by Daniel": Dn 7:13. See Simon Claude Mimouni, *Le Judaïsme anciens du VIᵉ siècle avant notre ère au IIIᵉ siècle de notre ère*, 637.

78 "what Josephus prudently": *Antiquities*, 18:23–24. An effective, though overly suggestive, general view can be found in Reza Aslan, *Zealot: The Lives and Times of Jesus of Nazareth* (New York: Random House, 2013), 63ff.

78 "an ardent love of liberty": *Antiquities*, 18:23.

81 "an inscription": Besides the texts specifically dealing with the epigraph that are mentioned in Sources and Historiography, see Lémonon, *Pilate et la gouvernement*, 15ff., and Bond, *Pontius Pilate*, 11ff.

82 "One recent hypothesis": Géza Alföldy, "L'iscrizione di Ponzio Pilato: una discussione senza fine?," in Gianpaolo Urso, ed., *Iudaea Socia – Iudaea Capta* (Pisa: Edizioni ETS, 2012), 137ff.; and the author's earlier work, "Pontius Pilate und das Tibereium von Caesarea Maritima," *Scripta Classica Israelitica* 18 (1999): 85ff.

83 "a judgment . . . by Philo": *Legatio ad Gaium*, 299–305.

83 "starkly negative view": *Legatio ad Gaium*, 301–2.

84 "in 41": see the indications in Sources and Historiography and notes to chapter 5.

86 "we owe to Josephus": *Wars*, 2:169–74; *Antiquities*, 18:55–59. See also Erwin R. Goodenough, *Jewish Symbols in the Greco Roman Period*, vol. 4 (New York: Bollingen Foundation, 1954), 11ff.

86 "You shall not make": Ex 20:4.

87 "a multitude": Josephus, *Antiquities*, 18:57—*katà plethyn*.

88 "according to Josephus": *Wars*, 18:166.

90 "Josephus offers us a . . . sequence": *Wars*, 2:175–77; *Antiquities*, 18:60–62.

92 "as the *Antiquities* seem to say": *Antiquities*, 18:62.

93 "Josephus quickly mentions": *Antiquities*, 18:63; and bear in mind also 20:200, which is much less well-known and debated.

94 "sixteenth-century criticism": I am thinking of Giuseppe Giusto Scaligero and of the Lutheran philology contemporary to him (Hubert van Giffen and Lucas Osiander): Emil Schürer, *Geschichte des Judischen Volkes im Zeitalter Jesu Christi*, 544ff.; and Robert Eisler *The Messiah Jesus and John Baptist according to Flavius Josephus' recently discovered "Capture of Jerusalem" and Other Jewish and Christian Sources*, translated by Alexander H. Krappe (New York: Dial Press, 1931), 36ff.

94 "reads more or less like this": Basically I accept the restitution of Bond, *Caiaphas*, 61 (and of others), in turn not distant from that of André Pelletier, "L'originalité du téimoniage de Flavius Josèphe sur Jésus," *Recherches de Science Religieuse* 52 (1964): 177ff. See also S. G. F. Brandon, *Jesus and the Zealots: A Study of the Political Factor in Primitive Christianity* (Manchester: Manchester University Press, 1967), 121ff.

95 "Tacitus also refers": *Annales*, 15:44:3. See Harald Fuchs, "Tacitus über die Christen," *Vigiliae Christianae* 4 (1950): 65ff., about which Alfons Kurfess, "Tacitus über die Christen," *Vigiliae Christianae* 5 (1951): 148–49.

95 "shared his source": the accuracy of Tacitus's information on the Judaic tradition—Syme, *Tacitus*, 467ff—makes the hypothesis very plausible.

3. GOD AND CAESAR

97 "The most detailed version": Jn 18:28–19:16a. It is a consolidated view that the fourth Gospel consists of two distinct parts: the account of Jesus's public life (1–12), and that of the Passion (13–20).

97 "some important historians sustain it": the classic formulation of the alternative is in Albert Schweitzer, *Geschichte des Leben-Jesu-Forschung* (Tübingen: J. C. B. Mohr, 1906), and is basically reproposed by Fergus Millar, "Reflections," 355, 399.

97 "which John calls": Jn 18:28.

97 "John says": 18:28.

98 "Roman criminal repression": the works of Santalucia point in the right

direction, and also contain further bibliography: Santalucia, "Lo portarono via"; Id., *Diritto e processo penale nell'antica Roma*, 2nd ed. (Milan, Giuffrè Editore, 1998), to which we can add Id., "Praeses provideat," in Mantovani and Pellecchi, eds., *Eparcheia, autonomia e civica Romana*, 69ff., especially 83; and also Anna Bellodi Ansaloni, "Riflessioni sulla condotta processuale di Gesù davanti a Pilato," in *Studi per Giovanni Nicosia*, vol. I (Milan: Giuffré, 2007), 443ff. Still useful is the old book of R. W. Husband, *The Prosecution of Jesus: Its Date, History and Legality* (Princeton: Princeton University Press, 1916), on which see G. A. Barton, "On the Trial of Jesus before the Sanhedrin," *Journal of Biblical Literature* 41 (1922): 205ff. As for studies of the theme by historians of Roman law, it is worth mentioning other essays in Amarelli and Lucrezi, and also the writings of Massimo Miglietta, *I.N.R.I. Studi e riflessioni intorno al processo a Gesù* (Naples: Satura Editrice, 2011). An essay which should also be kept in consideration is Pietro De Francici, "Brevi riflessioni intorno al processo di Gesù," in *Studi in onore di Giuseppe Grosso*, vol. 1 (Turin: Giappichelli, 1968), 4ff.

99   "What accusation . . . ?": Jn 18:29.

99   "If this man": Jn 18:30.

100   "We found this man": Lk 23:2 (translation modified).

100   "Take him yourselves": Jn 18:31.

101   "We are not permitted": Jn 18:31. Cohn, *The Trial and Death of Jesus*, 147.

101   "You shall not murder": Ex 20:13.

101   "*lex Iulia maiestatis*": Richard A. Bauman, *The Crimen Maiestatis in the Roman Republic and Augustan Principate* (Johannesburg: Witwatersrand University Press, 1970), remains an important work. See also Carlo Venturini, "La giurisdizione criminale in Italia e nelle province nel primo secolo," in Amarelli and Lucrezi, *Il processo*, 1ff.

102   "Are you the King of the Jews?": Jn 28:33.

103   "master of the world": as Antoninus Pius would say of himself, about a century and a half later: *egò mèn toû kósmou kýrios*, through the testimony of L. Volusius Mecianus, *ex <de> lege Rhodia*, in *Digesta* 14.2.9.

103   "Do you ask this?": John 18:34.

105   "Am I perhaps a Jew?": Jn 18:35 (translation modified).

108   "Jesus answered": Jn 18:36.

108   "My kingdom": Jn 18:36.

109   "as has been said": by Assmann, *Herrschaft und Heil* (*Potere e salvezza*, 3ff.).

110 "God himself ": Assmann, *Herrschaft und Heil* (*Potere e salvezza*, 40ff., 247ff.); Id., *Monotheismus und die Sprache der Gewalt* consulted in the Italian edition, *Non avrai altro Dio. Il monoteismo e il linguaggio della violenza* (Bologna: Il Mulino, 2007), 25ff.

110 "invented by Josephus": *Contra Apionem*, 2:16 (ed. Naber, vol. 6). In truth, his is only the first testified use of the word: that he invented it is a conjecture.

110 "theopolitics": the definition ("theopolitik") is by Martin Buber, "Das Königtum Gottes" (1932), in *Werke, 2, Schriften zur Bibel* (Munich: Kosel-Schneider, 1964), 485ff, especially 689ff.

111 "This transforms the One": What I say here presupposes an important book by Roberto Esposito, *Due: La macchina della teologia politica e il posto del pensiero*, especially 25ff., 61ff., 82ff. His interpretation is an acute and innovative development of a Hegelian theme: *Vorlesung über die Philosophie der Geschichte*, in *Werke (1832–45)*, edited by Eva Moldenhauer and Karl Marcus Michel (Frankfurt: Suhrkamp, 1972), in English as *The Philosophy of History*, translated by John Sibree (New York: Dover, 1956), 241ff., 275ff., 278ff.; and see, also by Hegel, *Religionphilosophie*, vol. 1, *Die Vorlesung von 1821*, edited by Karl-Heinz Ilting (Naples: Bibliopolis, 1978), 209ff., 517ff.

112 "The concept of 'political theology'": Schiavone, *Invention of Law*, 226ff.

113 "as has been elegantly sustained": by Assmann, *Herrschaft und Heil* (*Potere e salvezza*, 16).

113 "Archimedean point": Assmann, *Herrschaft und Heil* (*Potere e salvezza*, 22).

115 "Render to the emperor": Mk 12:13–17; Mt 22:15–22; Lk 20:20–26 (my translation). On the structure of Mark's text, which was a model for others: Wayne A. Meeks, *The Origins of Christian Morality: The First Two Centuries* (New Haven: Yale University Press, 1993), 74ff.

115 "a reading proposed long ago": A correct interpretation is offered by Massimo Cacciari, *Il potere che frena* (Milan: Adelphi, 2013), 54ff., where there are also other references. To be borne in mind: Oscar Cullmann, *Der Staat im Neuen Testament* (Tübingen: Mohr, 1956), in English as *The State in the New Testament* (New York: Charles Scribner's Sons, 1956).

117 "figures in it for essential reasons": Carl Schmitt, "Drei Möglichktein eines christliche Geschichtbildes," which appeared, with another title ("Drei Stufen historischer Sinngeburg"), in *Universitas* 8 (1950): 927ff.; Schmitt's observation relates to the Christian Creed (discussed in chapter 5), but the

context in which it appears clearly extends its scope: it is the very presence of Pilate in the Passion story that appears essential to the author.

117 "If . . . my followers": Jn 18:36.

118 "But about that day": Mt 24:36.

119 "in the Second Letter": 2 Thes 2:5–7 (ed. Merk).

120 "By opposition": My interpretation presupposes Cacciari, *Il potere*, especially 22ff., and Esposito, *Due*, 83ff. See also Massimo Cacciari and Roberto Esposito, "Dialogo sulla teologia politica," *Micromega* 2 (2014): 3ff. A different interpretation, which I do not share, is that of Oscar Cullman, *Christus und dei Zeit*, 3rd ed. (Zurich: EVZ Verlag, 1962), in English as *Christ and Time: The Primitive Christian Conception of Time and History*, translated by Floyd V. Filson (London: SCM Press, 1951; reprint 1957), 164ff.

120 "So you are a king?": Jn 18:37.

121 "You say": Jn 18:37.

123 "'superstition' . . . Tacitus": "exitiabilis superstitio": *Annales*, 15:44:3.

123 "Do you not hear . . . ?": Mt 27:13.

123 "He was interrogated": *Hermeneumata di Sponheim* (ed. Dionisotti), 2:73–77: "Reus sistitur latro, interrogatur secundum merita; torquetur . . ."

123 "What is truth?": Jn 18:38. Consideration should be given to Oswald Spengler, *Der Untergang des Abendlandes* (Munich: Beck'sche Verlagsbuchhandlung, 1923), in English as *The Decline of the West*, translated by Charles F. Atkinson, 2 vols. (London: George Allen & Unwin, 1926), 2:12, on which Agamben, *Pilate and Jesus*, 7ff. For a completely different perspective, see also Massimo Miglietta, "Est vir qui adest," in Cosimo Cascione and Carla Masi, eds., *Quid est veritas? Un seminario su verità e forme giuridiche* (Naples: Jovene, 2013), 277ff.

124 "Nietzsche": *Der Antichrist: Fluch auf das Christentum* (1895, ed. Schlechta 1956), in English as *The Anti-Christ*, in *Twilight of the Idols and The Anti-Christ*, translated by R. J. Hollingdale (London: Penguin, 1990), 174.

124 "annihilation": Nietzsche, *The Anti-Christ*, 174.

124 "as Nietzsche makes out": Nietzsche, *The Anti-Christ*, 174.

125 "he had said": Jn 14:5–7.

126 "I give you a new commandment": Jn 13:34, 15:12 and 17.

126 "the mystery of lawlessness": 2 Thes 2:6: *tò gàr mystérion . . . tês anomías*.

126 "Jesus added something further": Jn 15:13.

127 "Mark and Matthew": Mk 15:5; Mt 27:14.

128 "Have nothing to do": Mt 27,19.

128 "she is called Procla": see notes to chapter 5.

128 "in Josephus": see *Antiquities*, 18:81–83.

128 "in the apocryphal Gospel of Nicodemus": in 2:1.

128 "only by Luke": Lk 23:6–12: Joseph B. Tyson, "The Lukan Version of the Trial of Jesus," *Novum Testamentum* 3 (1959): 249ff., is still a useful work; see also Id., "Jesus and Herod Antipas," *Journal of Biblical Literature* 79 (1960): 239ff.; and Harold W. Hoehner, *Herod Antipas* (Cambridge, UK: Cambridge University Press, 1972), though not always reliable. The idea that it is an invention was already in Dibelius, "Herodes und Pilatus," 113ff., followed by Burkill, "The Condemnation of Jesus," 321ff., and Bond, *Pontius Pilate*, 149.

129 "Herod and Pilate became friends": Lk 23:12: see also notes to chapter 5.

4. THE DESTINY OF THE PRISONER

132 "I find no reason to condemn him": Jn 18:38 (my translation).

132 "You brought me this man": Lk 23:13–14 (translation modified).

132 "[calling] together the chief priests": Lk 23:13 (translation modified).

133 "The Synoptics report the episode": Mk 15:6–15; Mt 27:15–23; Lk 23:18–19 (with a rather disjointed account, because it evidently brusquely reconnects with Mark's version, previously abandoned in order to relate the episode of Herod); Jn 18:39–40.

133 "The most reliable hypothesis": Momigliano, "Ricerche sull'organizzazione della Giudea sotto il dominio romano," 79.

134 "trace . . . can be found in Matthew": Mt 27:17.

134 "the crowd": *tô óchlo*: Mt 27:15.

134 "decided whom to free": *òn éthelon*: Mt 27:15.

135 "notorious": Mt 27:16. See Richard A. Horsley with John S. Hanson, *Bandits, Prophets, and Messiahs: Popular Movements at the Time of Jesus* (Minneapolis: Winston, 1985).

135 "Mark and Luke": Mk 15:7; Lk 23:19.

135 "only for John": Jn 18:40.

135 "Hans Kelsen": *Vom Wesen und Wert der Demokratie* (Tübingen: Mohr, 1929), in English as *The Essence and Value of Democracy*, edited by Nadia Urbinati and Carlo Invernizzi Accetti, translated by Brian Graf (Lanham, MD: Row-

man & Littlefield, 2013), 79ff.; *Staatsform und Weltanschauung* (Tübingen: Mohr, 1933), in English as "State-Form and World-Outlook," in Ota Weinberger, ed., *Hans Kelsen: Essays in Legal and Moral Philosophy*, translated by Peter Heath (Dordrecht: D. Reidel, 1973), 95ff; "Absolutism and Relativism in Philosophy and Politics," *American Political Science Review* 42 (1948): 906ff.; "Foundations of Democracy," *Ethics* 66 (1955–56): 1ff.

136 "almost metaphysical": I have developed this point elsewhere: Aldo Schiavone, *Non ti delego: Perché abbiamo smesso di credere nella loro politica* (Milan: Rizzoli, 2013), 29ff.; Id., "Crise de la réprésentation et démocratie en Europe," *Incidence* 10 (2014): 57ff.; and Id., "Political Theory of Democracy from an Italian Perspective," in Stefan Grundmann and Jan Thiessen, eds., *Recht und Sozialtheorie im Rechtsvergleich / Law in the Context of Disciplines* (Tübingen: Mohr Siebeck, 2015), 69ff.

136 "in a brief segment of text": Jn 18:31, 36, 38; 19:7, 14.

136 "once when": Jn 19:6 (translation modified).

136 "and a second time": Jn 19:15.

137 "In Luke": Lk 23:1 (my translation).

137 "It is then related": Lk 23:4. Let's not forget that Luke also used the same word—*óchlos*—in relation to the Temple guard unit that had arrested Jesus the night before: it is highly probable that he is repeating the same term to indicate more or less the same number of men.

137 "Finally, Luke says": Lk 23:13 (translation modified).

137 "in Matthew": Mt 27:20.

137 "in Mark": 15:11. In Matthew, as in Mark, the word is again *óchlos:* the same one both employed, like Luke, to denote the participants in the arrest of Jesus. We can deduce from it that they were drawing on Mark for both the arrest and the Barabbas episodes, and that Mark's text was the first to give the word at the very least an ambiguous semantic sense, in the sphere of which there was certainly the possibility of indicating even quite small groups whose members were not individually identifiable.

138 "it has been suggested": see also Cohn, *The Trial and Death of Jesus*, 148ff.

139 "as a quick sentence in Mark": Mk 15:8: "the crowd came and began to ask Pilate to do for them according to his custom," namely that Pilate release a prisoner.

141 "In Luke": Lk 23:13, 20, 22 (translation modified).

141 "on this point follows Mark and Matthew": Mk 15:9–15; Mt 27:17–23.

142 "took some water": Mt 27:24–25.

142 "Gospel of Peter": in 1:1.

143 "the people [of Jerusalem] as a whole": Mt 27:25.

143 "so Matthew says": Mt 27:24.

144 "For John": Jn 19:1–4.

144 "According to Luke": Lk 23:16 (translation modified).

146 "In Mark and Matthew": Mk 15:15; Mt 27:26.

146 "imagination of Caravaggio": the picture I am referring to is in the Museo di Capodimonte in Naples.

147 "Hail, King of the Jews!": Jn 19:3.

147 "in Mark and Matthew": Mk 15:18; Mt 27:29.

147 "Look, I am bringing him out": Jn 19:4.

147 "Here is the man": Jn 19:5.

148 "as John recounts": Jn 19:4.

148 "Crucify him!": Jn 19:6. So too the Synoptics: Mk 15:13–14; Mt 27:22–23; Lk 23:21.

148 "Take him yourselves": Jn 19:6.

149 "We have a law": Jn 19:7.

150 "John recounts": Jn 19:8.

150 "Both Mark and Matthew": Mk 15:5; Mt 27:14.

151 "a holy man": Lellia Cracco Ruggini, "Imperatori e uomini divini (I–VI secolo)," in Peter Brown, Lellia Cracco Ruggini, and Mario Mazza, *Governanti e intellettuali: Popolo di Roma e popolo di Dio (I–VI secolo)* (Turin: Giappichelli, 1982), 9ff.

153 "Where are you from?": Jn 19:9.

154 "gave him no answer": Jn 19:9.

154 "Do you refuse to speak to me?": Jn 19:10.

155 "You would have no power over me": Jn 19:11 (translation modified).

156 "the whole passage": Jn 19:12–16a (translation modified).

157 "trying to": Jn 19:12: *ezétei apolŷsai autón.*

159 "If you release this man": Jn 19:12.

159 "friend of the emperor": Millar, *The Emperor in the Roman World,* 110ff.

160 "about which Philo informs us": *Legatio ad Gaium,* 160: see also notes to chapter 2; for the dating of this policy to the years between 28 and 31, see Lémonon, *Pilate et la gouvernement de la Judée,* 223, which I think should be accepted.

164 "Christian 'at heart'": see notes to chapter 5.

166 "sits 'on the judge's bench'": Jn 19:13.

166 "Here is your King!": Jn 19:14.

166 "Away with him! Crucify him!": *âron âron:* Jn 19:15.

166 "Pilate answers": Jn 19:15.

166 "a question mark": . . . *stauróso.*

166 "nor can it be hypothesized": this is the hypothesis advanced by Jean Colin, *Les villes libres de l'Orient gréco-romain et l'envoi au supplice par acclamations populaires* (Brussels: Latomus, 1965), 9ff.

167 "They reply": Jn 19:15.

167 "John then recounts": Jn 19:16.

167 "the soldiers": Jn 19:23.

167 "Jesus of Nazareth": Jn 19:19.

167 "The chief priests": Jn 19:21.

168 "What I have written": Jn 19:22.

168 "went to Pilate 'boldly'": Mk 15:43.

168 "According to Matthew": Mt 27:62–65.

5. INTO THE DARKNESS

170 "Anatole France": "Le procurateur de Judée," 877ff.

170 "A passage in Tertullian": Tertullian, *Apologeticum,* 21:24 (and see also 21:18): *Et omnia super Christo Pilatus, et ipse iam pro sua coscientia Christianus, Caesari tunc Tiberio nuntiavit.*

170 "Pliny's correspondence": *Epistulae* (ed. Schuster), 10:96 (97).

170 "during those years": these are the years in which Sejanus's anti-Jewish pressure was most forcefully exercised: see notes to chapter 4 and further on in this chapter.

171 "the beginning of this book": see Sources and Historiography, and chapter 1.

172 "did not bear images": *Legatio ad Gaium,* 299.

172 "it was now on everyone's lips": *Legatio ad Gaium,* 300.

172 "Don't set off a revolt!": *Legatio ad Gaium,* 301.

172 "concludes the letter": *Legatio ad Gaium,* 301–6.

173 "a fairly late dating": Lémonon, *Pilate et la gouvernement de la Judée,* 205ff.; Bond, *Pontius Pilate,* 45ff.

174 "*divi Augusti filius*": a good reconstruction is offered by Bond, *Pontius Pilate*, 37ff.

175 "in the eighteenth book": Josephus, *Antiquities*, 18:85–89.

176 "Josephus's portrayal of its inhabitants": *Antiquities*, 9:291.

177 "a massacre": *Antiquities*, 18:88: at least according to the Samaritans before the legate of Syria.

178 "a friend": *Antiquities*, 18:89.

178 "Luke talks of": Lk 13:1.

179 "of Jesus to Antipas": Lk 23:6–12: see chapter 3 and notes.

179 "Josephus recounts": *Antiquities*, 18:89.

180 "from Origen": *Contra Celsum* (ed. Koetschau), 2:34.

180 "to Eusebius": *Historia Ecclesiastica* (ed. Schwartz), 2:7.

180 "to Ambrose": *Expositio evangelii secundum Lucam* (ed. Adriaen), 22:63–23:25.

180 "to John Chrysostom": *Homiliae in Matthaeum* (ed. Field, in *Patrologia Graeca*), 86:1, 87:1.

180 "Augustine himself": *Sermones* (ed. Maurini, in *Patrologia Latina*), 214:7. See also *Enarrationes in Psalmos* (ed. Dekkers and Fraipont), 63:4:8.

180 "In one of these invented tales": *Tutti gli Apocrifi del Nuovo Testamento* (ed. Moraldi), "Ciclo di Pilato, Lettera di Tiberio a Pilato" (8 and 10), 741; M. R. James, *The Apocryphal New Testament: Being the Apocryphal Gospels, Acts, Epistles, and Apocalypses* (Oxford: Clarendon Press, 1924), 157; J. Armitage Robinson, "Apocrypha Anecdota II," in *Texts and Studies: Contributions to Biblical and Patristic Literature* (Cambridge, UK: Cambridge University Press, 1899), 78–81. A useful contribution is Gilbert Dagron, "Pilate après Pilate: L'Empire chretien, les juifs, les images," in Giacomo Jori, ed., *Ponzio Pilato: Storia di un mito* (Florence: Leo S. Olschki, 2013), 31ff. (but the whole volume is worth taking into consideration).

180 "According to another tradition": *Apocrifi* (ed. Moraldi), 726; James, *Apocryphal New Testament*, 158.

180 "known also to Eusebius": again in *Historia ecclesiastica*, 2:7.

181 "in the Lausanne region": *Apocrifi* (ed. Moraldi), 753; James, *Apocryphal New Testament*, 158.

181 "In yet another version": *Apocrifi* (ed. Moraldi), "Ciclo di Pilato, Paradosis di Pilato," (10), 750; James, *Apocryphal New Testament*, 155.

181 "writing his *Apology*": *Apology* (ed. Rauschen), 1, 35:9, and 48:3 (we are in the years around 155): Lémonon, *Pilate*, 250–51.

181 "The *Acts of Pilate*": Tischendorf, *Evangelia Apocrypha*, lxx–lxxi; *Apocrifi* (ed. Moraldi), 593ff. See also Edoardo Volterra, "Di una decisione del senato romano ricordata da Tertulliano", in *Scritti giuridici*, vol. 4 (Naples: Jovene, 1993), 419ff., especially 421ff.

182 "known as the 'Pilate Cycle'": which ties in with and completes the Gospel of Nicodemus: *Apocrifi* (ed. Moraldi), 725ff.; James, *Apocryphal New Testament*, 94ff.

183 "on the fabric of its early memory": an intriguing book on this topic is Paul Veyne, *Quand notre monde est devenu chrétien (312–394)* (Paris: A. Michel, 2007).

185 "the Nicene Creed": *Staurothénta te ypèr emôn epì Pontíou Pilátou* (ed. Dossetti, 1967)—"He was crucified for us under Pontius Pilate." Attention is rightly drawn to the presence of Pilate in this text by Giorgio Agamben, *Pilate and Jesus*, 1ff.

INDEX

Abraham, 69

Acts of Pilate, 170, 181–82

Aetius, 112

Agrippa I (Herod Agrippa), vassal
prince of the Romans in Judaea,
130, 172, 173, 174

Ain Arrub, 90

alétheia (truth), 121–26

Alexandria, Egypt, 83, 86

Ambibulus, Marcus, 56

Ambrose, 180

Annals (Tacitus), 95

Annas, 12, 13, 37–38, 39, 42, 44–45,
46, 96

   Pilate and, 40, 106, 127–28, 132–33

Antichrist, 120

Antiochus III (the Great), Seleucid
King of Syria, 68

Antiochus IV, Seleucid King of Syria, 70

Antipater, 72

Antiquities of the Jews (Josephus), 61, 74,
76, 86, 88, 90, 92, 93, 175–80

anti-Semitism, Jesus's death and, 142, 144

Antonia Fortress, 20, 24, 30, 32

Antony, Mark (Marcus Antonius), 72

Apamea, Peace of (188 BC), 68

apocalypse, 78, 118–20, 122, 126

Apollonius of Tyana, 151

Apology (Justin), 181

Aramaic, 102

Archelaus (Herod Archelaus), Ethnarch of Samaria, Judaea, and
Idumea, 74

Aristides, Aelius, 63

Aristobulus II, 71

Armenia, 57

Arthur, King, 9

Ascension of Jesus, 182

Asia, 66

Augustine (Aurelius Augustinus
Hipponensis), 113

   *Lectures on the Gospel according to
St. John,* 12

   Pilate and, 12, 180

Augustus (Gaius Julius Caesar Octa-
vianus Augustus), *princeps* of
Rome, 52, 174
  Herod the Great and, 73
  Roman administrative system and,
    54–55, 64–65
  Roman Judaea and, 74, 91
  Roman social hierarchy and, 53–54
  Tiberius and, 56, 57

Babylonian exile, 68, 73
Barabbas, 12, 133–41, 157, 158, 220*n*
basileús (king), 104
Bible, 114, 214*n*
  Jewish identity and, 21–22, 78–79,
    109–10, 141, 164, 174
  messianic theology and, 77–78
  monotheism and, 11, 108–9
  Pilate and, 105, 143, 174
  see also Gospels; New Testament
Bulgakov, Mikhail, 14, 51

Caesar, Julius, Judaea and, 71–72
Caesarea, 37, 52, 56, 57, 66, 68, 73,
  102
  Druseum at, 83
  Herod the Great and, 52, 73, 81, 83
  Jewish protest against idolatry in,
    87–88, 106
  Pilate epigraph and, 10, 81–83
  Roman administration and, 19, 22,
    24, 81, 93, 172
Caiaphas (Joseph):
  Jesus and, 12, 13, 37, 38, 39–40, 41,
    43–44, 47, 49, 96

Pilate and, 40, 79, 105, 127–28, 132–
  33, 171
Caligula (Gaius Julius Caesar Augus-
tus Germanicus), *princeps* of
Rome, 10, 171–72, 181
Campania, Italy, 53
Capri, 57, 58
Caravaggio, Michelangelo Merisi, 146
Christianity:
  Acts of Pilate and, 182
  anti-Semitism and, 142, 144
  beginnings of, 7, 12, 94, 95, 169
  Gospels and, 10–13
  Hellenism and, 70
  Jesus's kingship and, 112–13
  monotheism and, 111–13
  revolt of 66 and, 118
  role of worldly power and, 119
Chrysostom, John, 180
Cicero, Marcus Tullius, 53, 66, 84
Claudius (Tiberius Claudius Caesar
Augustus Germanicus), *princeps*
of Rome, 84, 86
concordia ordinum, 53
Constantinople, 185
consuls, 55, 61
Covenant, 108–9, 112, 114

Daniel, Book of, 77, 78
Dead Sea, 66, 77
democracy, Barabbas's freeing by
  "crowd" and, 135–36
Diaspora, 23, 68, 83, 95
Druseum, 83
Drusus, Decimus Claudius, 58, 83

Egypt, 11, 21, 61, 66, 105
England, 74
equestrians, 53–54, 56, 58, 61
Essenes, 74, 76–77
Eusebius, 113, 180–81

Feast of Unleavened Bread, 21
Flaccus, Pomponius, 60
France, 74
France, Anatole, 14, 170
freedmen, 53, 58
free will, predestination and, 164, 184

Gabbatha (Stone Pavement), 157
Gabinius, Aulus, 71
Galilee, 13, 21, 66, 73–74, 129, 130, 135, 172, 176
    Luke and, 178–79
Gaza, 66
Gellius, Aulus, 65
Germany, 57
Gethsemane, garden of, 27–29, 36, 38
Gospels, 119, 169, 183, 184
    Barabbas in, 133–39
    Gethsemane and, 27–29, 36
    Jesus's arrest and, 25–26, 29, 33–37, 40, 42–43, 44, 129, 211n
    Jesus's burial and, 168
    Jesus's condemnation and, 136, 141–42, 143, 144, 148, 156–67, 223n
    Jesus's death and, 10, 11–12, 93–94
    Jesus's flogging and, 144–49
    Jesus's imprisonment and, 37, 39, 41, 42, 43, 44–46, 47–50, 94, 96
    Jesus's innocence asserted by

    Pilate and, 132, 137, 141–42, 148, 153, 162
    Jesus's life and, 12
    Jesus's popularity and, 138
    Jesus's presentation by Pilate to the Jews and, 147–48
    Jesus's questioning by Pilate and, 97, 99, 100, 105, 106, 108, 115, 121, 123, 127–29, 132, 137, 141–42, 150, 160–62, 164, 221n
    Jewish authorities and, 40, 47
    Judas and, 33–35
    Last Supper and, 19–21, 27, 28
    Pharisees and, 75–76
    Pilate's washing of hands and, 141–42
    religious memory and, 10–13
Gratus, Valerius, 37, 39, 56, 57, 79
Greece, 11, 63, 66, 80, 120

Hadrian, *princeps* of Rome, 54, 65
Hasmonean dynasty, 69, 70–71
Hellenism, 69–70, 72–73, 75, 79
Herod Antipas, 12, 13, 73–74, 172, 182
    Jesus's condemnation and, 142
    Jesus's questioning and, 128–30, 179
Herodians, 74, 79, 115, 130, 133
Herod Philip, 73
Herod the Great, 21, 40, 74, 88, 90, 129
    Augustus and, 73
    Caesarea and, 52, 73, 81, 83
    Jerusalem palace of, 20, 24, 172
    Sadducees and, 72, 75
    Sanhedrin and, 72–73

history, religious memory and, 8, 9–13,
    19, 27, 28, 34, 67–68, 74–77, 103,
    104, 113, 144, 150, 160, 164, 183
ho ánomos (lawless one), 119–20
ho katéchon (one who now restrains),
    119–20, 126
Horace, 63
Hyrcanus II, Hasmonean king, 71, 72

Idumea, 21, 66, 72
Illyria, 57
imperium, 60–61
India, 11
Inquisition, 44
Isis, 58
Israel, people of, 21, 22, 47, 48, 50, 68,
    71, 77, 108–9, 110, 130, 163

James, Gethsemane and, 28
Jerusalem, 7, 66, 69, 178–79
    Antonia Fortress and, 20, 24, 30, 32
    "Cenacle" room in, 20
    Gareb hill in, 20
    Herod Antipas and, 129–30
    Herod's palace and, 20, 24, 172
    Jesus's arrival in, 24, 26
    Jesus's capture and interrogation by
        Sanhedrin in, 37–51, 94, 95, 96, 98,
        100, 104
    Jesus's popularity in, 138
    Jewish authorities and, 25–26,
        29–51
    Kidron and, 20
    Last Supper and, 19–21, 26–27, 28
    Mark Antony and, 72
    Mount of Olives and, 27

Pharisees and, 40, 75, 76
Pilate's aqueduct project and, 90–93,
    106
Pilate's testing of idol ban in, 86–90,
    106, 173, 174
Pompey and, 71, 91, 150
population of, 20
Praetorium in, 97, 103, 120, 131,
    139–40, 144, 146, 147, 153, 158,
    159, 165, 166
Roman destruction of, 9
Roman military and, 23–24, 30, 92
Stone Pavement (Gabbatha) in, 157
Temple of, 21, 24, 26, 41, 67, 71, 73,
    75, 80, 91, 92, 118
Jesus:
    Annas and, 42, 44–45, 46, 96
    apocalypse and, 118, 122, 126
    arrest of, 25, 26, 29–37, 40, 42–43, 44,
        80, 96, 98, 106, 125, 129, 132–33,
        162, 211n
    arrival in Jerusalem, 24, 26
    Ascension of, 182
    Barabbas exchange offer and, 133–
        41, 157, 158
    birth of, 129, 130
    Caiaphas and, 12, 13, 37, 38, 39–40,
        41, 43–44, 47, 49, 96
    condemnation of, 7, 13, 136–38,
        141–42, 143, 144, 145, 148, 156–67,
        169, 223n
    "crowd" and fate of, 134, 135–36,
        137–39, 141–44, 148, 221n
    crown of thorns and, 147
    death as accepted destiny of, 161–63,
        168, 184

death as ultimate expression of love and, 126–27

death of, 7, 10, 11–13, 93–94, 95, 139, 142, 144, 155, 156, 157, 158, 164, 167–68, 169, 173, 178, 182, 184, 185

doctrine of dual human and divine nature of, 111–16, 184, 218n

flogging of, 144–48, 149, 158, 165

Galilee and, 129, 130

Gethsemane and, 27–29, 36, 38

God's will and, 35, 36, 127, 155–56, 161, 162, 163, 168, 184

Herod Antipas and, 128–30, 142, 179

historical record and, 10

interrogation by Sanhedrin of, 37–51, 94, 95, 96, 98, 100, 104

inscription on cross of, 167–68

Jewish authorities and, 25–26, 29–33, 34, 35, 37, 38–50

Jewish culture and, 110

kingship and, 100, 101, 102–16, 120–21, 122, 147

language used by, 102

Last Supper and, 19–21, 26–27, 28

"love one another" command and, 126–27

Messianic nature of, 100

monotheism and, 111–13, 140–41, 218n

new Covenant and, 112

Nietzsche on, 124

personal magnetism of, 104

Peter's denial of, 42–43

Pharisees and, 76, 115

Pilate's power over, 154–55

Pilate's questioning of, 8, 96–130, 131, 146, 150, 153–56, 160–62, 163, 164, 165, 218–19n, 221n

religious and political charges and, 32, 42, 50, 100–101, 104

Resurrection of, 182

Second Coming and, 118–20, 126

traders driven from Temple and, 26

"trial" of, 38, 39, 41, 44, 49–50, 98

truth and, 121–26

Jewish Revolt of 66 AD, 70, 75, 77, 118, 135

Jews:

Babylonian exile and, 68, 73

Bible and identity of, 21–22, 78–79, 109–10, 141, 164, 174

calendar and, 20, 21

Diaspora and, 23, 68, 83, 95

exodus from Egypt and, 21

military service and, 23–24

responsibility for Jesus's death and, 139, 155, 156, 157, 158, 164, 167, 184

Roman policy and, 9, 22, 58–59, 86, 95, 171–72, 173, 174–75

Joan of Arc, 9

John, Gospel of, 10, 12, 24, 126, 183

Jesus-for-Barabbas offer in, 133, 135–36, 138

Jesus's arrest and, 28, 29–30, 35–36, 40, 44, 94

Jesus's burial and, 168

Jesus's condemnation and, 144, 148, 156–67, 223n

Jesus's flogging and, 146, 165

Jesus's imprisonment and, 37, 39, 41, 43, 44–46, 47, 50, 94

Jews (*continued*)
Jesus's presentation by Pilate to the Jews and, 147–48
Jesus's questioning by Pilate and, 97, 99, 100, 105, 106, 108, 115, 123, 127, 129, 132, 150, 160–62, 164
Judas and, 34
kósmos and, 112
Last Supper and, 21, 34
Pilate's assertions of Jesus's innocence and, 132, 141, 142, 148, 153, 162
Pilate's state of mind and, 150, 152, 153, 165
subjection of Pilate to Jesus's will and, 164, 167–68
Joseph of Arimathea, 12, 13, 168
Josephus, Flavius, 128
Antiquities of the Jews, 61, 74, 76, 86, 88, 90, 92, 93, 175–80
Caesarea and, 52, 81, 83
Hebraic world's religious differences and, 74–78
Jesus's death and, 10, 12, 93–94, 95
Jesus's imprisonment and, 37–38, 39
Jewish authorities and, 40
Judaean prefecture and, 56, 61
Pharisees and, 74, 75–76
Pilate and, 10, 12, 56, 83, 85, 86–94, 173, 175–80
Sadducees and, 74–75
theocracy and, 110, 218n
Wars of the Jews, 61, 74, 76, 86, 87, 90, 93, 175
Zealots and, 78
Judaea, kingdom of, 66, 68–74

Caesar and, 71–72
first Roman contact with, 68
Hellenization of, 69–70, 72–73
Herod the Great and, 20, 21, 40, 52, 72–73, 74, 75, 81, 83, 88, 90
Mark Antony and, 72
Pompey and, 71, 91, 150
toparchies in, 71
Judaea, Roman, 7, 9, 10, 13, 19, 21, 26, 37, 55, 60, 106, 171, 175
Caesarea as administrative center of, 19, 22, 24, 81, 93, 172
criminals and, 135
description of, 66–67
equestrian administration of, 53
establishment of, 74
Marcellus and, 178
messianic theology and, 77–78
religious memory and tensions in, 67–68, 74–77
revolt of 66 and, 70, 75, 77, 118, 135
Zealots and, 78
see also Jerusalem; Judaea, kingdom of; Pilate, Pontius
Judaism:
apocalypse and, 78, 118–20
Christianity and, 70
Covenant and, 108–9, 114
death penalty and, 101, 149
God's power and earthly violence in, 114, 163
Hellenism and, 69–70, 72–73, 75, 79
high priest and, 79–80
Jesus and, 110
Jesus's teachings and, 140–41
messianic theology and, 77–78

Passover and, 21, 41, 97, 101
Pilate and, 85, 93, 105, 123, 152, 174–75
religious differences and, 67–68, 74–78
Roman Empire and, 9, 22, 58–59, 71, 86, 91, 95, 150, 171–72, 173, 174–75
Sanhedrin and, see Sanhedrin
Seleucids and, 69–70, 77
theocracy and, 110, 112, 114, 149
washing of hands and, 142, 143
Judas Iscariot, 12
Jesus's arrest and, 33–35
Justin, (Martyr), 170, 181
Apology, 181

Kelsen, Hans, 135, 138
kósmos (worlds), 112

Lamia, Aelius, 60
Last Supper, 19–21, 26–27, 28, 34
dating of, 20–21
Latins, 53
Latium, Italy, 53
Lausanne, Switzerland, 181
Lectures on the Gospel according to St. John (Augustine), 12
Legatio ad Gaium (On the Embassy to Gaius) (Philo), 84, 171–75
Legions, Roman
III "Gallica," 23
VI "Ferrata," 23
X "Fretensis," 23
XII "Fulminata," 23
liberty, predestination and, 164, 184

literature, Pilate and, 14, 51, 170
Livia Drusilla, 58
Luke, Gospel of, 12, 26
Barabbas and, 135, 137, 220n
Galileans' executed by Pilate and, 178–79
Herod Antipas's questioning of Jesus and, 128–30, 179
Jesus in Gethsemane and, 27, 28, 29, 36
Jesus's flogging and, 144–45, 146
Jesus's imprisonment and, 41, 42, 47–48, 50, 96
Jesus's questioning by Pilate and, 97, 100, 132, 137, 141–42, 221n
Last Supper and, 19
Pharisees and, 76
Pilate's assertions of Jesus's innocence and, 132, 137, 141–42
see also Synoptics (Matthew, Mark, and Luke)

Marcellus ("friend" of Vitellius), 178
Mark, Gospel of, 12, 26
Barabbas in, 135, 137, 139, 220n
Gethsemane in, 28, 29, 36
Jesus's condemnation in, 144
Jesus's flogging in, 146
Jesus's imprisonment in, 41, 47, 48–50
Jesus's questioning by Pilate in, 97, 123, 127, 128, 150, 221n
Last Supper in, 19, 20
see also Synoptics (Matthew, Mark, and Luke)
Masada, 73

Matthew, Gospel of, 12, 26, 181
apocalypse in, 118
Barabbas in, 134, 139, 220n
crown of thorns in, 147
Gethsemane in, 28, 29, 36
Jesus's burial in, 168
Jesus's condemnation in, 142, 143, 144
Jesus's flogging in, 146
Jesus's imprisonment in, 41, 47, 49
Jesus's questioning by Pilate in, 97, 123, 127, 128, 150
Judas in, 34
Last Supper in, 34
mystery of lawlessness in, 119, 126
Pilate's assertions of Jesus's innocence in, 137, 141–42
Pilate's washing of hands in, 141–42
Second Coming in, 119
see also Synoptics (Matthew, Mark, and Luke)
Metamorphoses (Ovid), 151
monotheism, 11, 108–9, 111–13, 140–41, 218n
Moses, 69, 176, 177
Mount Gerizim, 176
Mount of Olives, 27
mystery of lawlessness, 119, 126

New Testament, 11
see also Gospels
Nicene Creed, 185
Nicodemus, Gospel of, 128, 181–82
Nietzsche, Friedrich, Pilate's questioning of Jesus and, 124
Nisan, 19, 20

Old Testament, 214n
On the Embassy to Gaius (Legatio ad Gaium) (Philo), 84, 171–75
Origen, (origenes Adamantius), 180
Ovid, 151

Palestine, 21, 25, 66, 75, 78, 91, 153
Parthians, 72
Passover, 21, 41, 97, 101, 157
pardoning custom at, 133–34
patricians, 53
Paul, 70, 113
Herod Agrippa I and, 130
mystery of lawlessness and, 119, 126
Pilate and, 12
Second Coming and, 119, 120
Second Letter to the Thessalonians and, 119
Peraea, 66, 74
peregrines, 53
Pesach, 21, 23
Peter, Gospel of, 142
Peter:
denial of Jesus and, 42–43
Gethsemane and, 28, 36
Petronius, Gaius, 151
Satyricon, 151
Pharisees, 40, 115
Gospels and, 75–76
Josephus and, 74, 75–76
Pilate and, 75, 76, 88, 174
Sanhedrin of Jerusalem and, 80
Philip (Herod Philip), 73
Philo of Alexandria:
Legatio ad Gaium (On the Embassy to Gaius), 84, 171–75

Pilate and, 10, 83–86, 90, 105, 171–75, 177

Sejanus and, 59, 160

Pilate, Pontius:

Annas and, 40, 106, 127–28, 132–33

apocryphal writings and, 170, 180, 181–82

aqueduct project and, 90–93, 106

Augustine and, 12, 180

background of, 52–53, 56

behavior and motivations and, 8

Bible and, 105, 143, 174

Caesarea epigraph and, 10, 81–83

Caiaphas and, 40, 79, 105, 127–28, 132–33, 171

end of historical record of, 180

gilded shields incident and, 172–73, 174

Gospels and, *see* Gospels; *specific books of the New Testament*

Herod Antipas and, 128–30, 179, 182

historical record vs. religious memory and, 9–13

idolatry and Roman standards and, 86–90, 106, 173, 174

inscription on Jesus's cross and, 167–68

Jerusalem and, 19, 20, 22–24, 25, 86–93; *see also* Jerusalem

Jesus's acceptance of death and, 164, 167–68, 184

Jesus's arrest and, 25, 26, 29–33, 36–37, 40, 98, 106, 132–33

Jesus's burial and, 168

Jesus's condemnation and, 7, 13, 142, 143, 148, 156–67, 169, 223n

Jesus's death and, 12, 13, 94, 95, 167–68, 169, 185

Jesus's exchange for Barabbas and, 133–41, 157, 158

Jesus's flogging and, 144–48, 149, 158, 165

Jesus's innocence asserted by, 132, 137, 141–42, 145, 148, 153, 162

Jesus's kingship and, 100, 101, 102–16, 120–21, 122, 147

Jesus's personality and, 104, 122–23, 127, 131, 150–53, 154, 162

Jesus's presentation to the Jews by, 147–48, 149, 157

Jesus's questioning by, 8, 96–130, 131, 132, 146, 150, 153–56, 160–62, 163, 164, 165, 218–19n

Jesus's silences and, 123, 153, 154

Jewish authorities' attempted intimidation of, 158, 159–60, 165, 170–71

Josephus and, 10, 12, 56, 83, 85, 86–94, 173, 175–80

Judaean prefecture and, 7, 10, 52, 56, 57, 59–65, 83–95, 132, 159, 169, 171–78, 212–13n

Judaism and, 85, 93, 105, 123, 152, 174–75

languages and, 102

legends and, 180–81

literature and, 14, 51, 170

military background and, 56–57, 177

Nietzsche on, 124

personality of, 83, 85, 89–90

Pharisees and, 75, 76, 88, 174

Pilate, Pontius (*continued*)
  Philo of Alexandria and, 10, 83–86, 90, 105, 171–75, 177
  power over Jesus and, 154–55
  powers and duties of, 61–65, 213–14n
  praenomen and, 52, 82
  return to Rome and, 178, 179–80
  Sadducees and, 75, 88, 99, 174
  Samaritan repression and, 175–79
  Sanhedrin and, 47, 48, 50, 51, 100, 105, 132–33, 136–38, 145, 165, 167, 168, 169, 170–71, 172–73, 174
  Sejanus and, 58–59
  superstition and, 151
  Tertullian on, 170, 171, 180, 181, 184
  Tiberius and, 56–57, 58, 59, 82, 159, 170–71, 172–73, 174–75, 181, 182, 185
  truth and, 123, 125
  view of in early Christianity, 183–85
  Vitellius and, 40, 60, 176–79
  washing of hands and, 141–42, 143
  "where are you from?" inquiry and, 153–54, 165
  wife of, 128, 181
"Pilate Cycle," 182
Piraeus, 52
plebeians, 53
Pliny, 170
political theology, 112
  see also theocracy
Polybius, 63, 120
Pompey the Great, 71, 91, 150
Posidonius, 67
Praetorian Guard, 58

Praetorium, 97, 103, 120, 131, 139–40, 144, 146, 147, 153, 158, 159, 165, 166
praetors, 55, 61
predestination, free will and, 164, 184
prefects, powers and duties of, 61–65
princeps, 56, 60, 61, 64, 159
Procla, 128, 181
proconsuls, 60, 61
propraetors, 61
Psalms, 71, 214n

Quirinius, Publius Suplicius, 37
Qumran, 77

Revolt of 66 AD, Jewish, 70, 75, 77, 118, 135
Rhodes, 58
Rhône River, 181
Roman Empire:
  administrative system and, 54–55
  Christianity's rise in, 183–85
  citizen rights and, 62, 64
  criminal law and, 64–65, 98, 123, 129
  death penalty and, 101
  Essenes and, 76–77
  imperial vs. senatorial provinces in, 55
  imperium and, 60–61
  inclusive and integrative nature of, 22, 62, 65–66, 80, 100
  Judaism and, 9, 22, 58–59, 71, 86, 91, 95, 150, 171–72, 173, 174–75
  legal system and, 62–65

Mediterranean East and, 9, 13, 22–23, 66, 69

Praetorian Guard and, 58

religion and, 9, 22, 58–59, 86, 95, 171–72, 173, 174–75, 183

revolt of 66 and, 70, 75, 77, 118, 135

Seleucids and, 68–69

self-identity and, 22

Senate and, 55, 72

social and political hierarchies and, 53–54

superstitions and, 151

taxation and, 62, 72, 91, 100, 101, 115

torture and, 123

Zealots and, 78

Romans, 53

Romulus, 9

Rufinus, Tyrannius, 181

Rufus, Annius, 56

Sadducees, 13, 37, 40

Barabbas and, 135

Hellenism and, 75, 79

Herod and, 72, 75

Josephus and, 74–75

people's relations with, 137

Pilate and, 75, 88, 99, 174

Sanhedrin of Jerusalem and, 80

Samaria, 21, 66, 135

Pilate's repression in, 175–79

Samaritan council, 176, 177

Sanhedrin, 13, 29, 32, 71, 80, 91

Barabbas and, 135, 136, 137–38, 139–41

death penalty and, 101, 149

Herod the Great and, 72–73

Jesus's condemnation and, 136–38, 145, 149–50

Jesus's imprisonment and, 37–51, 94, 95, 96, 98, 100, 104

Pilate and, 47, 48, 50, 51, 100, 105, 132–33, 136–38, 145, 165, 167, 168, 169, 170–71, 172–73, 174

Satyricon (Petronius), 151

Scaevola, Quintus Mucius, 112

scribes, 76, 80

Sebaste, 66, 73

Second Coming of Christ, 118–20, 126

Sejanus, Lucius Aelius, 174

anti-Jewish policy and, 58–59, 160, 173, 175, 223n

death of, 173

Philo of Alexandria and, 59, 160

Pilate and, 58–59

Tiberius and, 59

Seleucids, 68–70, 72, 77

Senate, Roman, 55, 72

senators, 53–54, 60

senatusconsults, 58

senatus populusque (senate and people), 106

Sicily, 66

slaves, 53

Solomon, 71, 214n

Spinoza, Baruch, 112

Strabo, 55

Straton's Tower, 52

Suetonius, 58

Synoptics (Matthew, Mark, and Luke), 21, 24, 28, 29
  Barabbas and, 133–39, 220n
  crown of thorns and, 147
  Jesus's burial and, 168
  Jesus's condemnation and, 141–42, 143, 144
  Jesus's flogging and, 144–45, 146
  Jesus's imprisonment and, 39, 41, 43, 46–50, 94, 96
  Jesus's questioning by Pilate and, 97, 100, 115, 121, 123, 127–29, 132, 137, 141–42, 150, 221n
  Pilate's assertions of Jesus's innocence and, 132, 137, 141–42, 148
  Pilate's washing of hands and, 141–42
  subjection of Pilate to Jesus's will and, 164
  see also specific Synoptic Gospels
Syria, 23, 37, 40, 55, 60, 71, 105, 159, 165, 176–79

Tacitus, Cornelius, 171
  Annals, 95
  Jesus's death and, 10, 12, 95
  Pilate and, 59–60
  Tiberius and, 58
taxes, taxation, 62, 72, 91, 100, 101, 115
Temple of Jerusalem, 21, 24, 26, 41, 67, 71, 73, 75, 80, 91, 92, 118
Tertullian, 113, 170, 171, 180, 181, 184
theocracy, 110, 112, 114, 149, 218n
Thessalonians, Second Letter to the (Paul), 119

Thomas, 125
Tiberius (Julius Caesar Augustus), princeps of Rome, 10, 55, 95
  Augustus and, 56, 57
  Caesarea and, 82
  Capri and, 57, 58
  death of, 180
  military campaigns and, 56–57
  personality of, 57–58
  Pilate and, 56–57, 58, 59, 82, 159, 170–71, 172–73, 174–75, 181, 182, 185
  Rhodes and, 58
  Sejanus and, 59
Tiber River, 181
Tirathana, Samaria, 176
toparchies, 71
Torah, 70, 75, 76, 80, 89
torture, Roman law and, 123
Trinity, Holy, 11, 125
truth, love as, 126–27

Ulpian (Domitius Upianus), 61, 63–64

Varro, Marcus Terentius, 112
Vienne, France, 181
Vitellius, 40, 60, 176–79

Wars of the Jews (Josephus), 61, 74, 76, 86, 87, 90, 93, 175
washing of hands, 141–42, 143

Zealots, 78